# GOD'S
## DARK CLOUDS

# GOD'S LIGHT ON DARK CLOUDS

Theodore L. Cuyler

THE BANNER OF TRUTH TRUST

THE BANNER OF TRUTH TRUST
3 Murrayfield Road, Edinburgh EH12 6EL, UK
P.O. Box 621, Carlisle, PA 17013, USA

\*

First published 1882
First Banner of Truth Edition 2008

ISBN: 978 1 84871 023 8

\*

Typeset in 10.5/15 pt Sabon Oldstyle at
The Banner of Truth Trust, Edinburgh

Printed in the USA by
Versa Press, Inc.
East Peoria, IL

\*

This new Banner edition contains a number of footnotes
that help to explain a few historical allusions in the text that
would have been obvious to the original readers.

TO THE

DESPONDING AND BEREAVED

THESE WORDS OF SYMPATHY AND CHEER

ARE LOVINGLY INSCRIBED

# CONTENTS

*In the autumn of 1881, 'the four corners of my house were smitten' again with a heart-breaking bereavement in the death, by typhoid fever, of our second daughter, Louise Ledyard Cuyler, at the age of twenty-two, who possessed a most inexpressible beauty of person and character. Her playful humour, her fascinating charm of manner, and her many noble qualities drew to her the admiration of a large circle of friends, as well as the pride of our parental hearts. After her departure I wrote, through many tears, a small volume entitled God's Light on Dark Clouds, with the hope that it might bring some rays of comfort into those homes that were shadowed in grief. Judging from the numberless letters that have come to me I cannot but believe that, of all the volumes which I have written, this one has been the most honoured of God as a message-bearer to that largest of all households—the household of the sorrowing.*

THEODORE L. CUYLER
*Recollections of a Long Life: An Autobiography*

## God's Light on Dark Clouds

*T*o-day as I sit in my lonely room, this passage of God's Word flies in like a white dove through the window: 'And now men see not the bright light which is in the clouds; but the wind passeth and cleanseth [or cleareth] them.' To my weak vision, dimmed with tears, the cloud is exceeding dark, but through it stream some rays from the infinite love that fills the throne with an exceeding and eternal brightness of glory. By-and-by we may get above and behind that cloud into the overwhelming light. We shall not need comfort then; we want it now. And for our present consolation God lets through the clouds some clear, strong, distinct rays of love and gladness.

One truth that beams in through the vapours is this: God not only reigns, but he governs his world by a most beautiful law of compensations. He sets one thing over against another. Faith loves to study the illustrations of this law, notes them in her diary, and rears her pillars of praise for every fresh discovery. I have noticed that the deaf often have an unusual quickness of eyesight; the blind are often gifted with an increased capacity for hearing; and sometimes when the eye is darkened and the ear is closed, the sense of touch becomes so exquisite that we are able to converse with the sufferer through that sense alone. This law explains why God put so many of his people under a sharp regimen of hardship and burdenbearing in order that they may be sinewed into strength; why a Joseph must be shut into a prison in order that he may be trained for a palace and for the premiership of the kingdom. Outside of the Damascus Gate I saw the spot where Stephen was stoned into a cruel death; but that martyr's blood was not only the 'seed of the Church', but the first germ of conviction in the heart of Saul of Tarsus. This law explains the reason why God often sweeps away a Christian's possessions in order that he may become rich in faith, and why he dashes many persons off the track of prosperity, where they were running at fifty miles per hour, in order that their pride might be crushed, and that they might seek the safer track of humility and holy living. What a wondrous compensation our bereaved nation is receiving for the loss of him who was laid the other day in his tomb by the lakeside! That cloud is already raining blessings, and richer showers may be yet to come.[1]  God's

---

[1] A reference to the death of the 20th President of the United States, James Garfield, who died on September 19, 1881 as the result of an assassin's

people are never so exalted as when they are brought low, never so enriched as when they are emptied, never so advanced as when they are set back by adversity, never so near the crown as when under the cross. One of the sweetest enjoyments of heaven will be to review our own experiences under this law of compensations, and to see how often affliction worked out for us the exceeding weight of glory.

There is a great want in all God's people who have never had the education of sharp trial. There are so many graces that can only be pricked into us by the puncture of suffering, and so many lessons that can only be learned through tears, that when God leaves a Christian without any trials, he really leaves him to a terrible danger. His heart, unploughed by discipline, will be very apt to run to the tares of selfishness and worldliness and pride. In a musical instrument there are some keys that must be touched in order to evoke its fullest melodies; God is a wonderful organist, who knows just what heart-chord

---

gunshot received the preceding July. He was buried at Lake View Cemetery in Cleveland, Ohio. What is less clear is what the subsequent 'blessings' referred to are. It is just possible that this may mean the administration of President Chester A. Arthur, Garfield's Vice President, who became President on his death. Arthur overcame many obstacles to reform the civil service, to the extent that publisher Alexander K. McClure wrote, 'No man ever entered the Presidency so profoundly and widely distrusted, and no one ever retired . . . more generally respected.' Author Mark Twain, deeply cynical about politicians, conceded, 'It would be hard indeed to better President Arthur's administration.' See also the reference to this in the penultimate paragraph of 'Right Seeing'. *Ed.*

to strike. In the Black Forest of Germany a baron built a castle with two lofty towers. From one tower to the other he stretched several wires, which in calm weather were motionless and silent. When the wind began to blow, the wires began to play like an Æolian harp in the window. As the wind rose into a fierce gale, the old baron sat in his castle and heard his mighty hurricane-harp playing grandly over the battlements. So, while the weather is calm and the skies clear, a great many of the emotions of a Christian's heart are silent. As soon as the wind of adversity smites the chords, the heart begins to play; and when God sends a hurricane of terrible trial you will hear strains of submission and faith, and even of sublime confidence and holy exultation, which could never have been heard in the calm hours of prosperity. Oh, brethren, let the winds smite us, if they only make the spices flow; let us not shrink from the deepest trial, if at midnight we can only sing praises to God.

If we want to know what clouds of affliction mean and what they are sent for, we must not flee away from them in fright with closed ears and bandaged eyes. Fleeing from the cloud is fleeing from the divine love that is behind the cloud. In one of the German picture-galleries is a painting called 'Cloudland'; it hangs at the end of a long gallery, and at first sight it looks like a huge repulsive daub of confused colour, without form or comeliness. As you walk towards it the picture begins to take shape; it proves to be a mass of exquisite little cherub faces, like those at the head of the canvas in Raphael's 'Madonna San Sisto'. If you come close to the picture, you see only an innumerable company of little angels and cherubim! How often the soul that is frightened by trial sees nothing but a confused and repulsive mass of broken expectations and crushed hopes! But if that soul, instead of fleeing away into unbelief and despair, would only draw up near to God, it would soon discover that the cloud was full of angels of mercy. In one cherub-face it would see 'Whom I love I chasten.' Another angel would say, 'All things work together for good to them that love God.' In still another sweet face the heavenly words are coming forth, 'Let not your heart be troubled; believe also in Me. In my Father's house are many mansions. Where I am there shall ye be also.'

To-day my lonely room is vocal with such heavenly utterances. God's ways are not my ways, but they are infinitely better. The cloud is not so dense but love-rays shine through. In time the revealing 'winds shall clear' away the dark and dreadful mystery. Kind words of sympathy steal into the shadowed room of suffering. If Christ does not come in visible form to our Bethanys, he sends his faithful servants and handmaidens with words of warm, tender condolence. The fourteenth chapter of John never gleams with such a celestial brightness as when we read it under the cloud. No cloud can be big enough to shut out heaven if we keep the eye towards the throne. And when we reach heaven and see the cloud from God's side it will be blazing and beaming with the illumination of his love. The Lamb which is in the midst of the throne shall be our Shepherd, and shall guide us to fountains of waters of life, and God shall wipe away every tear from our eyes.

**2**

## BURNING THE BARLEY-FIELD

*A* great many precious spiritual truths lie concealed under the out-of-the-way passages of God's Word, like Wordsworth's

> violet by a mossy stone,
> Half hidden from the eye.

If we turn up a certain verse in the fourteenth chapter of the Second Book of Samuel, we shall find such a truth hidden under a historical incident. The incident is on this wise. Absalom, the artful aspirant to his father's throne, wishes to have an interview with Joab, the field marshal of David's army. He sends for Joab to come to him, but Joab refuses. Finding that the obstinate old soldier pays no heed to his urgent request, he practises a stratagem. He says to one of his servants: 'See! Joab's field is next to mine, and he hath barley there. Go and set it on fire!' And Absalom's servant set the field on fire. Then Joab arose and came to Absalom.

Now, just as the shrewd young prince dealt with Joab in order to bring him unto him, so God employs a regimen of discipline very often in order to bring wayward hearts to himself. Many a reader of this article may have had his barley-field set on fire; there are some even now whose fields are wrapped in flames or are covered with the ashes of extinguished hopes. With backsliders this method is often God's last resort. He sees that the wayward wanderers care more for their earthly possessions than they do for his honour or his service. So he touches them in the tenderest spot, and sweeps away the objects they love too well. They have become idolaters, and he sternly dashes their idols to atoms.

There was a time when our nation had shamefully backslidden from the fundamental principles of our Declaration of Independence. The value of cotton crops outweighed the value of liberty. The righteous God saw that we cared more for the perpetuity of our Union and our prosperity than we did for the rights of four millions of his children. But when the first flash of a national conflagration lighted up the southern sky, then millions of affrighted voices began to cry out, 'Why is our magnificent Union given to the flames?' We could sleep while God's law of right was trampled under foot; but when the national peace and power and pride were trodden down by the same remorseless heel, we awoke, as a man awakes at the cry of 'fire' under his own roof-tree. God saw what we prized most, and he touched that.

In like manner, many an individual sinner finds his way to Christ by the light of a burning barley-field. Sometimes the awakening comes in the shape of a bodily chastisement. The impenitent heart has never been moved by sermons and never been brought to repentance by any sense of gratitude for God's mercies. So the all-wise One sends a sharp attack of sickness, in order to reach the diseased and hardened heart. The sinner is laid on his back. He is brought to the very verge of eternity. As a past life of transgression rises before his conscience, and the terrors of a wrath to come seize upon him, he cries out, 'God be merciful to me a sinner!' When he recovers his health, and goes back into a world that looks very different to him now, his grateful song is, 'It was good for me to have been afflicted, for I had gone astray; my feet had wellnigh slipped.' I honestly believe that many a sick-bed has delivered the sufferer from a bed in perdition. Pain often drives to prayer. The door that shuts a man out from the world shuts him in to reflection, and finally into the ark of safety. 'There it is', said a young man, as he pointed to a diseased limb, which was eating away his life; 'and a precious limb it has been to me. It took me away from a career of folly. It brought me to myself, and to this room of trial where I have found Christ. I think it has brought me a great way on the road to heaven.' It was the testimony of a Christian who had lost his eyesight, after a long confinement to a dark room, 'I could never see Jesus until I became blind.'

We sometimes wonder why God takes one of his ministers out of the pulpit and lays him on a bed of dangerous illness. It is to give the man a look over the verge. He gets shorter views of life and of eternity. Three weeks on the couch of pain and peril teach him some things which he never learned in three years at a theological seminary. Sharp bodily affliction, even if it does not endanger life, is often a wholesome process. Paul's thorn in the flesh, Robert Hall's excruciating pains, and Richard Baxter's physical sufferings were a very expensive part of their education; but they graduated with higher honour and a brighter crown. Fiery trials make golden Christians. When the balsam-trees in God's garden are cut deep with the knife, they emit the sweetest gums.

During the last five years a great many barley-fields have been consumed. Brother A— had his fortune swept away in the commercial conflagration of 1873; but his heavenly hope was locked up in what was more fire-proof than any iron safe, and his Christian character came out like pure gold from the flames. One of the most benevolent and useful Christian merchants in America has lately seen the flames of ruin go through his field of barley, and the earnings of an honest life are ashes! He has an inheritance left yet which the Rothschilds could not buy;[1] and the very loss of his stocks and 'securities' has led him to inventory afresh the blessed treasures which he has been laying up in heaven. So, from being a bankrupt, he finds that his best investments are untouched; and there has been no depreciation in his real estate, which lies very near to the everlasting throne.

God often sees that a career of unbroken worldly prosperity is becoming very fatal to the soul. Therefore he puts the torch to the barley-field. Not only are the impenitent thus dealt with, to bring them to consider their ways, but his own children are often put through a process which is marvellously improving to their graces, for a career of rapid success is seldom healthful to piety. Very few even of Christ's choice ones can travel life's railway with perfect safety at forty miles per hour. The heated axle is very apt to snap, or else the engine flies the track of conformity to God and goes off the embankment.

Prosperity brings out only a few of a good man's graces; it often brings out a great many secret lusts, and no little pride, and selfishness, and forgetfulness of the Master. When a favourable wind strikes a vessel 'right aft', it only fills a portion of the sails; when it veers round and strikes it 'on the beam', then every inch of canvas is reached.

[1] An international banking and finance dynasty of German Jewish origin with established operations across Europe. Ennobled by the Austrian and British governments, the name is still synonymous for extreme wealth. *Ed.*

Good reader, if the Lord is so shifting the winds that they reach your undeveloped graces of humility and faith and patience and unselfish love, do not be alarmed. He does not mean to swamp you, or send you on a lee shore; he only intends to bring you into a 'better trim' and give you a more abundant entrance into the desired haven.

Count up all the worldly losses you have had, and see if you are not the gainer, if these losses have but sent you closer to your Saviour. You have less money, perhaps, but more enjoyment of the treasures you found at the cross. You are richer toward God. Perhaps there is a child the less in that crib now empty, but there is a child the more in glory; and when the Shepherd took your lamb he drew you nearer to him and to the fold on high. Our loving God has a purpose in every trial. If any heart-broken reader of these lines is crying out like Joab, 'Wherefore hast thou set my field on fire?' I beseech you not to flee away from God in petulant despair. He is only burning up your barley to bring you closer to himself. Let the flames light you to the mercy-seat. The promises will read the brighter. It is better to lose the barley than to lose the blessing.

3

## Weeping and Working

*T*he smallest verse in the Bible is one of the largest and deepest in its heavenly pathos. 'Jesus wept.' What mysterious meanings may have lain behind those tears, no one need try to fathom; but, for one, I prefer to see in them the honest expression of grief for a friend who was dead, and of sympathy for two heart-broken women. Christ's power displayed at that sepulchre overwhelms me; it was the power of a God. But his pity touches me most tenderly; it was the pity of a man. Those moistened eyes are my elder brother's. The sympathy that walked twenty miles to Bethany, that drew him to those desolate women, that started the tears down his cheeks and choked his voice with emotion—that sympathy links us to him as the sharer and the bearer of our own sorrows. There is something vicarious in those tears, as there is in the precious blood shed on the cross a few days afterwards. His love seems to 'insert itself vicariously right into our sorrows', and he takes the burden right into his own heart.

But it was a practical sympathy. Had our Lord come to Bethany and taken the two bereaved sisters into their guest-chamber and had a 'good cry' with them, and then gone away and left Lazarus in his grave and them in their grief, it would have been all that our neighbours can do for us when we are in a house of bereavement. But it would not have been like Jesus. He did not come to Bethany simply to weep. He came there to work a marvellous miracle of love. He wept as a man; he worked as the Lord of power and glory. He pitied first, and then helped. The same love that moistened his eyes moved his arm to burst open that tomb and bring the dead Lazarus to his feet. A few days afterwards he wept for sinners, and then wrought out salvation for sinners by his own agonies on the cross. Is there no lesson for us in this? What are tears of sympathy worth if we refuse to lift a finger to help the suffering or to relieve distress? And what a mockery it is to weep over the erring and do nothing to save them! Only when we 'bear one another's burdens' do we 'fulfil the law of Christ.'

There is another connection that weeping has with working. We relieve our own suffering hearts by turning the flood of grief upon some wheel of practical activity. An eminent minister of God who was under peculiar bitter trial, once said to me, 'If I could not study and preach and work to the very utmost, I should go crazy.' The millstones grinding upon themselves soon wear themselves away to powder. But useful occupation is not only a tonic, it is a sedative to the troubled spirit. Instead of looking in upon our own griefs until we magnify them, we should rather look at the sorrows of others, in order to lighten and lessen them.

The poor fisherman, in one of Sir Walter Scott's romances, says to the lady who comes to his cottage after the death of his child: 'You rich folk when ye are in trouble may sit wi' yer handkercher to yer een, but we puir bodies maun off to our work agen, even tho' our hearts are thumpin' like a hammer.' If the poor fellow had only known it, he was a great deal better off at his honest work than if he had been idly nursing his grief with the 'handkercher to his een'. Some of the best work ever done for the Master is wrought by his servants when the 'hammer' of affliction is not only beating away on the heart, but is breaking down selfishness and unbelief. When sorrow is allowed to settle in the soul, it often turns the soul into a stagnant fen of bitter waters, out of which sprout the rank rushes of self-will and unbelief and rebellion against God. If that same sorrow is turned outward into currents of sympathy and beneficence, it becomes a stream of blessings. A baptism of trial is often the best baptism for Christ's service. If tears drive us to toil, then toil will in turn drive away tears, and give us new and sacred satisfactions. When our blessed Saviour wept, it was on the eve of his mightiest works, once in raising the dead, and once in redeeming a dying world. Weeping and working may even blend profitably together; for the chiefest of Christ's apostles tells us that during three busy years of his life he ceased not to warn perishing sinners, night and day, with tears.

> Since Thou on earth hast wept,
> And sorrowed oft alone,
> If I must weep with Thee,
> My Lord, Thy will be done!

4

## Short Views

*A*mong the manifold improvements in the Westminster Revision, we are happy to find that our Lord's discourse against sinful worrying is given in the right English.[1] Our common version of the closing portion of the sixth chapter of Matthew has always been very misleading to the average reader. Christ never commanded us to 'take no thought for the morrow'; such counsel would contradict common sense, rational prudence, and other explicit commands in the Bible. What our Lord so emphatically forbade was sinful anxiety, or the overloading of today's work with worry about the day that has not yet come. The revisers have hit the nail exactly on the head by introducing the word 'anxious' into a half-dozen verses of that portion of the Sermon on the Mount. 'Be ye not anxious for your life what ye shall eat . . . Which of

[1] A reference to the work of British scholars, who met regularly at the Deanery of Westminster, London, and which led to the publication of the *Revised Version* of the Bible (NT 1881; complete Bible 1885; ASV 1901).*Ed.*

you by being anxious can add one cubit to the measure of his life?' This whole remonstrance against borrowing trouble in advance is summed up in the happily translated sentence, 'Be not therefore anxious for the morrow; for the morrow will be anxious for itself.'

We may be sure that our blessed Lord knew what was in man when he gave so much space in his sermon to this one tormenting sin, and repeated six times over his entreaties to avoid it. Worry is not only a sin against God, it is a sin against ourselves. It sometimes amounts to a slow suicide. Thousands have shortened their lives by it, and millions have made their lives bitter by dropping this gall into their souls every day. Honest work very seldom hurts us; it is worry that kills. I have a perfect right to ask God for a strength equal to the day, but I have no right to ask him for one extra ounce of strength for tomorrow's burden. When tomorrow comes, grace will come with it, and sufficient for the tasks, the trials, or the troubles. God never has built a Christian strong enough to stand the strain of present duties and all the tons of tomorrow's duties and sufferings piled upon the top of them. Paul himself would have broken down.

There is only one practical remedy for this deadly sin of anxiety, and that is to take short views. Faith is content to live 'from hand to mouth', enjoying each blessing from God as it comes. This perverse spirit of worry runs off and gathers some anticipated troubles and throws them into the cup of mercies and turns them to vinegar. A bereaved parent sits down by the new-made grave of a beloved child and sorrowfully says to herself, 'Well, I have only one more left, and one of these days he may go off to live in a home of his own, or he may be taken away; and if he dies, my house will be desolate and my heart utterly broken.' Now who gave that weeping mother permission to use the word 'if'? Is not her trial sore enough now without overloading it with an imaginary trial? And if her strength breaks down, it will be simply because she is not satisfied with letting God afflict her; she tortures herself with imagined afflictions of her own. If she would but take a short view, she would see a living child yet spared to her, to be loved and enjoyed and lived for. Then, instead of having two sorrows, she would have one great possession to set over against a great loss; her duty to the living would be not only a relief to her anguish, but the best tribute she could pay to the departed.

That is a short view which only takes in immediate duty to be done, the immediate temptation to be met, and the immediate sorrow to be carried. My friend, if you have money enough today for your daily wants and something for God's treasury, don't torment yourself with the idea that you or yours may yet get into an alms-house. If your children cluster around your table, enjoy them, train them, trust them to God, without racking yourself with a dread that the little ones may some time be carried off by the scarlet fever, or the older ones may yet be ill married or may fall into disgrace. Faith carries present loads and meets present assaults and feeds on present promises, and commits the future to a faithful God. Its song is:

> Keep Thou my feet; I do not ask to see
> The distant scene; one step's enough for me.

We shall always take that one step more wisely and firmly and successfully if we keep our eye on that only. The man who is climbing the Alps must not look too far ahead, or it will tire him; he must not look back, or he gets dizzy; he has but to follow his guide, and set his foot on the right spot before him. This is the way you and I must let Christ lead, and have him so close to us also that it will be but a short view to behold him. Sometimes young Christians say to me, 'I am afraid to make a public confession of Christ, I may not hold out.' They have nothing to do with holding out; it is simply their duty to hold on. When future trials and perils come, their Master will give them help for the hour, if they only make sure that they are his. The short view they need to take is a close, clear view of their own spiritual wants, and a distinct view of Jesus as ever at hand to meet those wants. If the fishermen of Galilee had worried themselves over the hardships they were to encounter, they might have been frightened out of their apostleships and their eternal crowns.

We ministers need to guard against this malignant devil

of worry. It torments one pastor with a dread lest, if he preach certain truths boldly, he may offend his rich pew-holders and drive them away. Let him take care of his conscience, and his master will take care of him. Another is worried lest his cruse may run dry and his barrel fail. But his cruse has not yet run dry. Oh no, it is his faith that is running low. Some of us, at the beginning of a year's work, are tempted to overload ourselves with the anticipation of how much we have to do; we need not worry if we will only remember that during the whole year there will be only one working day, and that is—today. Sufficient to each day is the labour thereof.

Once more we say—let us take short views. Let us not climb the high wall till we get to it, or fight the battle till it opens, or shed tears over sorrows that may never come, or lose the joys and blessings that we have, by the sinful fear that God will take them away from us. We need all our strength and all the grace God can give us for today's burdens and today's battle. Tomorrow belongs to our heavenly Father: I would not know its secrets if I could. It is far better to know whom we trust, and that he is able to keep all we commit to him until the last great day.

# 5

## FLOWERS FROM THE TOMB OF JESUS

O ur Lord was crucified in the season of early flowers. During the month Nisan (or April) the winter rains made vegetation leap forth into wondrous beauty. The gardens were brilliant with the crocus and the hyacinth, and the plains of Sharon were snowy with the white narcissus. Jesus was buried in a rich man's garden, and no one can tell how many flowers and odorous vines had been planted by the gardener round Joseph's family tomb. The spices within and the plants without may have made the spot in which our dear Master slumbered exceeding fragrant.

That hallowed tomb was itself buried up centuries ago, and the very spot cannot be identified. But there are certain flowers of grace which will bloom upon the grave of Jesus to the end of time. Faith grows there in beautiful profusion. A sad company of ignorant doubters were those disciples in regard to their Master's resurrection; even when the three women came back from the sepulchre and pronounced it empty, and that they had seen the Saviour alive, some of the apostles treated it as an 'idle tale and believed it not'. Thomas stood out until an actual sight of his Lord silenced his unbelief. From that day faith in Christ's victory over death has been a cardinal feature in every Christian's creed. With it is linked that other faith that if Jesus rose again, so would every one who 'sleeps in Jesus' rise also from the dust. This perennial flower of faith, which blooms like certain roses, in all seasons, has been set out on innumerable graves all over our death-cursed world. It grows on the little mound that covers my dear boy; I seem to see it all over among the hillocks of Greenwood.[1]

Hope is another fragrant flower that springs from the burial sod. On one leaf of the plant we read, 'I am the resurrection and the life; he that believeth in me, though he were dead *yet shall he live.*' On another leaf is inscribed, 'Sorrow not as others that have no hope; for if Jesus died and rose again, even so them also which sleep in Jesus will God bring with him.' The expectation of every pastor, that he shall yet 'break ground' and ascend with his flock, cheers his soul when he stands beside the grave

---

[1] Cuyler lost two sons in infancy, Georgie in 1867, aged four-and-a-half years, from scarlet fever, and Mathiot in 1874, just twelve days old. Both were buried in Greenwood Cemetery, Brooklyn, New York, near where Cuyler served as minister of Lafayette-Avenue Presbyterian Church for over thirty years during the latter half of the 19th century. See also the additional notes at the end of the book. *Ed.*

in which his faithful ones are being laid, dust to dust.
This hope is an anchor that has held many a poor heart-
broken mother who has moistened her darling's resting
place with her tears. To her Jesus draws nigh and says,
'Weep not; this child shall rise again.' And so she tills that
little sacred soil until it is covered over with the blossoms
of hope as thick as white lilies of the valley. The original
seeds of this fair flower came from Christ's tomb in the
garden. It grows best when it is watered by prayer. That
is a desolate grave indeed over which there does not creep
out a single sprig or blade of hope!

Are these all the flowers which thrive in the hallowed
mould in which Christ's successors lie? No! There is one
modest lily called Resignation. Jesus himself declared that
it was better that he should have died, for he said that he
'*ought* to have suffered and to enter into his glory'. His
road to glory lay through the tomb, and so must ours.
Never did our Lord set this world above the better world.
He only brought three persons back to life (that we read
of), and then only for a high and special purpose to be
gained. There is a legend that the first thing Lazarus said
after his resurrection was, 'Shall I have to die again?' On
being told that he must, it is said that he never smiled
afterward. Truly, if some of the crowned ones in paradise
were driven back to this sin-stained earth, they might well
wear mourning for their own bereavement. To die is gain!
That is the sweet word which I detect in every bud and

leaf on the plant of Resignation. God has better things in store for us; his will, not ours, be done.

It may seem a strange place to set out the flower of Thankfulness; but that, too, grows and emits its sweetness from Christ's sepulchre and those of his followers. Paul, standing by that grave over which Jesus had triumphed, shouts aloud, '*Thanks* be to God who giveth us the victory through Jesus Christ our Lord.' His triumph over death is our triumph. Because he rose and lives again, we shall live also.

Not only on Easter Sabbaths are these flowers to be found on our Lord's emptied sepulchre, but every day, in every clime, wherever death hollows a grave, these precious plants of grace may be made to bloom, and to scatter their delicious perfumes. Perhaps some sorrowing child of God may read these lines and inquire, 'Where shall I go to find faith and hope, and resignation for yonder freshly piled mound over my dead?' We answer, Go to the tomb where Jesus vanquished death—in the garden.

6

## Trusting God in the Dark

*S*ometimes we have an experience in life that seems like walking through a long dark tunnel. The chilling air and the thick darkness make it hard walking, and the constant wonder is why we are compelled to tread so gloomy a path, while others are in the open day of health and happiness. We can only fix our eyes on the bright light at the end of the tunnel, and we comfort ourselves with the thought that every step we take brings us nearer to the joy and the rest that lie at the end of the way. Extinguish the light of heaven that gleams in the distance, and this tunnel of trial would become a horrible tomb. Some of us are passing through just such an experience now. We can adopt the plaintive language of the Psalmist and cry out: 'Thy hand presseth us sore; as for the light of our eyes, it also is gone from us; we are ready to halt, and our sorrow is continually before us.'

One of the most trying features of our trial is that we cannot discover the 'why' or the 'wherefore' of our special afflictions. Our heavenly Father did not consult us before the trial came, and he does not explain to us why he sent it. His ways are not our ways, nor his thoughts our thoughts; nay, they are the very opposite. The *mystery* of the providence perplexes and staggers us. For example, I open my daily journal, and read that the Bishop of Jerusalem, whom I left a few months ago in the prime of vigorous health, and wide usefulness, is cut off in the midst of his days. All his preparatory training for his office by eighteen years of missionary life comes to naught. This very day I am called for the sixth time in a few years to bury the dead from a certain Christian household. This time it is the head of the house that is taken, and the children are left to an orphanage. Beside me now sits a mourning mother, whose aching heart cannot understand why a beloved child is snatched away when she seemed the most indispensable to the happiness of the home. Every week a pastor has to confront these mysteries in the dealings of a God of love. To the torturing question, 'Why does God lead me into this valley of the shadow of darkness?' we can only reply, 'Even so, Father, for so it seems good in thy sight.' We are brought into the tunnel, however we shrink back. There is no retreat; we have nothing left to us but to grasp the very hand that brought us there and push forward. Like Bunyan's pilgrim, we can only say, 'I see not but that my road to heaven lieth through this very valley.'

Just in such trying hours it is that the adversary assails us most fiercely. He stirs up in our hearts bitter thoughts against God. He points us to the actual and realized loss, and tells us that heaven is utterly unseen, and no one comes back to assure us of its reality. And so he endeavours, with devilish suggestions, to blow out such lamps of divine promise as we have, to shatter every staff that we carry, and to make the pathway of trial more dark and desperate than before. This is not fancy; it is the actual trial to which the faith of thousands of God's people is at this moment subjected. Under these severe experiences more than one Christian has been sorely tempted to turn infidel, and to 'choose death rather than life'.

To my own mind there is only one solution for these mysteries and only one support for these days of terrible affliction. The only relief I can find is in the certainty that this life is not the end, but simply the *preparatory school* for the real and the endless life that is beyond. The moment that I accept this truth fully and hold it firmly, I find solid ground for my feet and light for my sorrowing soul. Then I discover that the whole journey of the believer is 'portioned out' to him, and that the dark tunnel on the road is just as surely appointed wisely as is the most flowery mead or the happiest walk over the 'Delectable Mountains'. Nay, more, when we reach heaven, we may discover that the richest and deepest and most profitable experiences we had in this world, were those which were gained in the very roads from which we shrank back with dread. The bitter cups we tried to push away contained the medicines we most needed. The hardest lessons that we learn are those which teach us the most and best fit us for service here and glory hereafter. It is the easiest thing in the world to obey God when he commands us to do what we like, and to trust him when the path is all sunshine. The real victory of faith is to trust God in the dark and through the dark. Let us be assured of this, that, if the lesson and the rod are of his appointing, and that his all-wise love has engineered the deep tunnels of trial on the heavenward road, he will never desert us during the discipline. The vital thing for us is, not to deny and desert him.

Let us also keep in mind that the chief object of the discipline is to develop character and to improve the graces of his children. Whom he loves he chastens, and corrects every son whom he receives. Every branch that bears not fruit he *prunes* it, that it may bring forth more fruit. 'Why do you cut that pomegranate-bush so cruelly?' said a gentleman to his gardener. The answer was, 'Because it is all running to useless leaves, and I want to make it bear.' Ah! it is a keen knife that our divine gardener employs, and he often severs the very heart-strings by his discipline; but *'afterward* it yieldeth peaceable fruit unto them that have been exercised thereby, even the fruit of righteousness.' God has a great many crucibles for his gold, where he may refine it. There is so much alloy of pride and self-will, or covetousness, or sinful idolatry in genuine Christians that they require the 'fining-pot' and the furnace. Sometimes prosperity is tenfold more damaging to us than sharp adversity. A fit of sickness may do more for soul-health than years of bodily strength and comfort.

To all my readers who are wondering why a loving God has subjected them so often to the furnace, my only answer is, that *God owns you and me,* and he has a right to do with us just as he pleases. If he wants to keep his silver over a hot flame until he can see his own countenance reflected in the metal, then he has a right to do so. It is the Lord, it is my loving teacher, it is my heavenly Father; let him do what seemeth him good. He will not lay on one stroke in cruelty, or a single one that he cannot give me grace to bear. Life's school-days and nights will soon be over. Pruning-time will soon be ended. The crucibles will not be needed in heaven.

So, to all my fellow-sufferers who are threading their way through the tunnels of trial, I would say: 'Tighten your loins with the promises, and keep the strong staff of faith well in hand. Trust God in the dark. We are safer with him in the dark than without him in the sunshine. He will not suffer your foot to stumble. His rod and his staff never break. Why he brought us here we know not now, but we shall know hereafter. At the end of the gloomy

passage beams the heavenly light. Then comes the exceeding and eternal weight of glory!

# 7

## God's School, and Its Lessons

*A*certain grey-haired pupil in the school of his heavenly Father once said, 'O God, thou hast *taught* me from my youth.' His experience in that school had been very remarkable, from his early beginnings among the sheep-cotes of Bethlehem. Constantly seeking instruction, he had prayed, 'Teach me thy statutes', 'Teach me thy way', 'Teach me to do thy will.' Sharp schooling had he received in those days of humiliation when a traitor-son drove him out of Jerusalem. Terrible punishment did he bring upon himself once when 'lust brought forth sin, and sin brought forth death', in the crime against Uriah. But had David not been under the instruction and discipline of the Holy Spirit, we never would have had many of the richest, profoundest, and most majestic Psalms—many of their most piercing wails and of their most jubilant thanksgivings.

That same school in which David was a pupil nearly thirty centuries ago is open yet. The term-time is as long as life lasts. It has its recreations and its rewards and its medals of honour, but no vacations. School is never 'out' until death comes to the door and beckons the pupil away. And oh! how happy many a scholar has been when the messenger has said to his heart, 'Now, my child, you have learned the hard lessons, and have finished your course; now you may *come home.*'

Of this wonderful school God himself is the Principal or Superintendent. The supreme purpose of it is to form character and to fit the immortal soul for the after-life of eternity. If there is no immortality of being, and if 'death ends all', then this world is an utter failure, and what we call providence becomes an unintelligible jargon. The moment we recognize the fact that this life is only a training-school to fit us for a coming world, that the Bible is its infallible text-book and the Holy Spirit its instructor and the Lord of glory its all-wise and all-loving head, then dark things become light, seemingly crooked things become straight, and mysteries become plain. If I am only a scholar, I must submit to the rod for my own correction, and remember who has appointed it. If I am only a scholar, I must spell out the hard lessons and submit to the sharp tasks, even though the pages of my diary be often blotted with tears; the things that I understand not now, I 'shall know hereafter,' when I have graduated into heaven.

My divine Teacher seems to have two great methods in this earthly school of his—instruction and discipline.

I am utterly ignorant and terribly wayward, therefore I need both; and they often blend together. Part of my instruction I get from his wondrous Word, and it is very inspiring and fascinating. A part I receive from the Holy Spirit's work, and it is very sanctifying. But no part of our schooling costs so dearly or yields such gracious fruits as the process of chastisement. The most famous teacher in Philadelphia, in his day, once said to a rich, indulgent father, 'You must take your boy out of my school if you are not willing to have me chastise him; he and the school too will be ruined if I have no *discipline*.'

Our heavenly teacher conducts his training-school for the very salvation of his scholars, and thus for his own honour and glory. The very word 'disciple' (*discipulus*) signifies a little scholar. The first essential to discipleship of the Lord Jesus was the willingness to deny self and to bear a cross at his bidding. That principle runs through all the deepest, richest Christian experience, and will do so, I suppose, to the end of time. Often when the hard lesson starts the tears, and the aching heart cries out in anguish, the hands of the dear Master point up to the words: 'As many as I love, I rebuke and chasten: be zealous therefore, and repent.' 'Whom the Lord loveth he chasteneth, and scourgeth every son whom he receiveth . . . No chastening for the present seemeth to be joyous, but grievous: nevertheless *afterward* it yieldeth the peaceable fruit of righteousness.' It is the 'afterward' that justifies the rod and reconciles us to the stroke. Grand old Richard Baxter exclaimed after a life of hard toil and constant suffering, 'O God, I thank thee for a bodily discipline of eight and fifty years.' Paul was indulging in no hypocritical cant when he said, 'I rejoice in tribulation.' God's ripest and most royal scholars are made such by an expensive education. His brightest gold comes out of the hottest furnace.

In this school of grace he employs many tutors. Sometimes he employs Poverty, which does for the soul what it did for the minds of such hard-faring youths as Hugh Miller[1] and James A. Garfield, it sinews the strength and develops force. More than one Christian who was getting too prosperous for his spiritual good has been turned over to this severe tutor, and he has sent him down to an humbler bench. As the purse was emptied, the soul grew richer in humility, and began to bear the fruits of the Spirit.

Another of God's tutors is Disappointment; and some of the best lessons in life are taught us by that stern-visaged schoolmaster. One of his lessons is that this world was not made solely for us, and our loss is often another man's gain. A second lesson is that our losses are often the very richest blessings. We had 'devised a way' for ourselves, and it would have led to certain danger. God

[1] Hugh Miller (1802-56) a self-taught geologist and writer, folklorist and evangelical Christian from humble background in the north of Scotland. *Ed.*

could not have sent a severer judgment on us than to let us have our own way; so he sent disappointment to drive us back. We cried out bitterly at first, but by-and-by we saw what we had escaped, and blessed the hand that had smitten us in the face. If I ever reach heaven, I shall feel like rearing a monument there of gratitude to the stern-visaged old tutor who so often helped me on by putting me back, and stripped me that I might travel heavenward the lighter and the freer.

Ah, brethren, this is a marvellous school which divine wisdom has opened, and a Father's love is superintending! He never spares the rod when the child is in danger of being spoiled. His pruning-knife cuts deep, but the clusters of grapes are all the larger and the sweeter. When Michelangelo saw a block of marble lying in the dirt, he said, 'There is an angel in that marble, and I will bring it out.' His hammer and chisel struck hard and deep, till the angel came forth. God's hammer of trial, blow on blow, brings out such angels as Faith, and sweet-visaged Peace, and strong-limbed Patience, and Sympathy, and the Love that has the likeness of Jesus Christ.

This school of God will soon close for us; the term-time is shortening every hour. Let us not shirk a lesson, however hard, or wince under a rod of chastisement, however sore and heavy. The richer will be the crown if we endure to the end and graduate into glory. What a promotion will that be for hearts that so often ached, and for eyes that so often wept, and for the faith that so often bled under the blow—to be lifted into the magnificent inheritance of the saints in light!

# 8

## GOD'S UNFOLDINGS

*S*itting today in Christ's school (for that is an essential idea of his church), let me say a few words to my fellow-scholars. The meek and the teachable will he guide in his way. There is room for us all in that spot where Mary sat—at the feet of Jesus. And the encouragement to us is: 'Call unto me, and I will answer thee, and show thee great and mighty things which thou knowest not.' This does not mean everything, even though our hearts may ache to find out many mysteries. The 'secret things belong unto God.' Over certain doors the inscription is affixed 'No admittance here.' In heaven we may know these things even as we are known; but now they are wisely hidden from our eyes.

Yet our all-wise and loving God is constantly unfolding himself to his earthly children. All scientific discovery is the passage from the unknown into the known; every truth discovered is a fresh unfolding of the Creator. Very slowly, very gradually is this progress effected. Centuries passed away before Galileo found out the rotation of the earth, and Newton the law of gravitation. Other generations must roll by before man learned enough about God's laws of electromagnetism to fashion the ocean telegraph. Yet these laws were all in existence in the days of Noah and Abraham; only they had not yet been unfolded. I once spent a night on Mount Righi, and there was nothing visible for a view from my window. But when the morning broke, the icy crowns of the Jungfrau and the Schreckhorn began to glitter in the early beams. They had been there all the night, waiting for the unfoldings of the dawn. Even so have all God's laws of the material universe and all his purposes of redeeming mercy through Jesus Christ been in existence from the beginning. They only waited for the dayspring of discovery. And one of the most delightful occupations of a devout mind is to watch the unfoldings of God, and to drink in new truths as he gradually reveals them.

The more closely I study my Bible, the more I detect a steady progress of divine doctrine, from the first line of Genesis to the closing grandeur of the Apocalypse. That little altar of turf on which Abel lays his lamb points onward to Calvary. The whole Jewish dispensation goes on step by step until the Messiah comes. Then I find four sections of the Book which photograph the life of Jesus to me, each one presenting some particular view of my Saviour's face and footsteps, and miracles and teachings.

Calvary and the resurrection only prepare the way for the descent of the Holy Spirit. Then comes the visible manifestation of the gospel in the conversation and organization of the primitive church. Peter's tongue, and Paul's brain, and John's heart, and Dorcas' needle all get into motion. These new converts require spiritual instruction, and the whole series of inspired epistles are produced. The man or the minister who asserts that the writings of the four evangelists are 'Bible enough for him' and that the epistles of Paul are only excellent surplusage, worthy of small attention, simply writes himself down an ignoramus. There is as veritable an unfolding of heavenly truth in the eighth chapter to the Romans as in the Sermon on the Mount. And when the laws of our spiritual life have been unfolded in the inspired epistles of Paul, John, Peter, and James, then the magnificent panorama of the Apocalypse is unrolled, and we get a glimpse of Christ's final triumphs and the glory of his celestial kingdom. After John lays down his pen, history takes up hers, and carries us on through the martyrdoms of saints and the councils and the conflicts and the Reformation period and the inauguration of modern missions to the nations who sit in darkness. At the foot of every page she writes, 'The earth is the Lord's, and the fulness thereof.'

In no direction do we behold more wonderful unfoldings of God than in what we call his Providence. This is a department of God's school in which we are learning fresh lessons every day. In Providence, divine wisdom is married to divine love. All things work together for good to them who love God and trust him. The sceptic jeers at this, but the trusting Christian knows it from actual experience. It is often a dear-bought experience, for some of God's truths are knocked into us by hard blows, and some lessons are spelled out through eyes cleansed with tears. Our perverse mistake is that we demand that God shall explain himself at every step, instead of waiting for him to unfold his intricate purposes at his own time and in his own way. Why A— is set up and good Brother B— (who seems equally deserving) is cast down; why the only little crib in one Christian home is emptied by death, and the nursery in another home is full of happy voices; why one good enterprise prospers and another one is wrecked—all such perplexing puzzles shake terribly the faith that is not well grounded on the Rock.

To all these pitiable outcries the calm answer of our heavenly Father is: 'Be still, and know that I am God. I lead the blind by a way they know not. What I do thou knowest not now, but thou shalt know hereafter.' These are the voices of love which come to us from behind the cloud. If we wait patiently, the cloud will break away or part asunder, and our eyes will behold the rainbow of mercy overarching the throne. Twenty years ago, on a day of thick fog and storm, I ascended Mount Washington by the old bridle-path. Over the slippery boulders we picked our toilsome way, unable to see anything but our surefooted horse and our guide. A sulky company were we when we reached the 'Tip-top House'. But presently a strong wind swept away the banks of mist, and revealed the magnificent landscape from the mountain's base to the great wide sea. As the wonderful vision unfolded itself to our delighted eyes, we could mark the pathway by which we had been led up to that mount of discovery. Tenfold more delightful was the outlook because we had gained it by such hard toil and it had been so long hidden from our sight.

That day's experience was a sermon to my soul. It taught me afresh just how a believer must leave God to order his footsteps, and how he must wait for God to unfold the hidden purposes of his love. Faith's stairways are steep and slippery. They can only be climbed by a sure foot and a steady hold on the unseen hand. In the hard clamber we are often thrown down on our knees. Cry as loudly as we may in the driving mist for 'more light', we do not receive any other answer than this: 'Fear not! *Only trust!*' If we unloose our hold on God's hand for an instant, we go over the precipice. But the more tightly we cling, the steadier we walk; the more willing we are to be humbled, the more certain are we to get upward; the more crosses we bear for Christ, the lighter will be our hearts; and by-and-by we shall reach that gate of pearl, the opening of which will unfold to us the everlasting flood of glory. These are among the thoughts which came into my mind as I have sat today in Christ's school, while some of the scholars around me have been singing; but, alas! some others are sobbing and weeping.

9

## Christ Sheperding His Flock

O ne of the most beautiful improvements of the new Revision of the Testament is that which makes the seventeenth verse of the seventh chapter of the Revelation to read thus: 'The Lamb which is in the midst of the throne *shall be their Shepherd,* and shall guide them unto fountains of waters of life.' This carries on into the heavenly world one of the most tender and profound relations which Jesus bears to his redeemed followers. To us, in our land and times, this oriental figure loses much of the vividness that it has to one who visits Palestine and sees a Judean shepherd among his flock. He is the master of a household of sheep—as much attached to his fleecy friends as daily intercourse and nightly watchings and personal exposures for them could make him. He searches out fresh pasturage for them; if a sheep is caught in a thicket, he hastens to rescue it; if a lamb falls into a swollen torrent, he is at hand to lift it out; if a wild beast shows himself at night near the sleeping flock, the shepherd seizes club or crook and gives him battle. Not only the savage beast, but the Bedouin robber must sometimes be encountered. Dr Thomson, in his *Land and Book,* says that one faithful fellow, between Tabor and Tiberias, instead of fleeing, actually fought three Bedouins, until he was hacked to pieces with their *khanjars,* and died among the sheep he was defending.

'I am the good shepherd. I lay down my life for the sheep.' This is the supreme act of his devotion to his flock. To analyse the theology of the atonement is for most believers as difficult as an attempt to analyse the maternal feeling before a mother who has just given the parting kiss to a dying daughter. The Christian's heart understands the atonement better than the Christian's head. It is a difficult doctrine for the brain, but a sweet and simple one to the affections. Jonathan Edwards himself could not apprehend the atonement one whit more clearly or feel it more intensely than the dairyman's daughter, when she sang to herself:

> How glorious was the grace
> When Christ sustained the stroke
> His life and blood the Shepherd pays,
> A ransom for the flock.

True faith simply believes what Jesus said, and rests implicitly on what Jesus did for us and will do for us to the end. This is the core of my practical theology, and so it is with millions of others. All we were but sheep going astray, and God has laid on him, the divine Shepherd, the iniquities of us all. This tells the whole story as to the ground of my hope for salvation; this, too, establishes such a relation between me and my Shepherd, that I am under supreme obligation to follow him wherever he leads. If we ever expect to be guided by him to fountains of waters of life in heaven we must learn here to submit to his guidance completely.

Three things our beloved Shepherd assures us. The first one is, 'I know mine own sheep.' He does not recognise them by any church-mark, for some persons may hide an unbelieving, unrenewed heart beneath a false profession; others, who never have enrolled themselves in any visible church-membership, may belong to the blood-bought flock. Jesus recognised the penitent sinner through her tears as distinctly as he saw through Judas behind his treacherous kiss. It is a precious thought to a true believer, however obscure in lot or however overlooked or misunderstood by others—'My Master knows me. He has me on his heart. He is a brother to my griefs. He knows what pasture I require; yes, and he understands when I need the chastising stroke. He detects my sins; therefore let me be watchful against temptation. He sees all my tears or my heartaches; therefore let me be cheerful under sharp trials.'

The second thing our Shepherd assures us is: 'Mine own know me.' This knowledge is gained by a sacred instinct. His own know him by the witness of the Spirit that witnesses with their spirits. How do I know my mother? By somebody else's description of her, by her picture, by an analysis of her mental qualities? No; I know her by the instincts of love. I have tested her sweet fidelities. I believe in her both for what she is to me and what she has done for me. The sincere Christian has a heart-knowledge which is gained by being sought out by the Shepherd, saved by the Shepherd, and by trusting and following the Shepherd. Of this experimental knowledge no scoffer can outwit him and no enemy can rob him. He has heard Christ's voice when he 'calls his own sheep by name and leads them out'. No one can counterfeit that voice. Sometimes in Palestine or Syria a stranger will try to mimic the shepherd's call; but the flock pay no heed to it. As soon as the genuine voice is heard, every head is up and the flock is in motion.

The third thing that Jesus assures us is, that 'He goeth before his sheep, and they follow him.' Ah, what pathways of trial he sometimes appoints to us! Never has he promised us an easy road or a smooth road, or such a road as our selfishness may select. He never consents that the flock shall decide as to the lot in which they shall be pastured, or over what deep hills he shall conduct them, or through what valleys of the death-shade they shall walk, listening to his voice through the dark. More than once faith stumbles and falls, but he lifts up and restores. Sometimes the burden breaks us down; but he says tenderly, 'Cast that burden on me.' Sometimes we cry out in anguish for some lost treasure of heart and home; but his firm reply is, 'Your treasure I will take care of. *Follow me.*' Whom he loves he chastens, and in proportion to the love is the discipline. The trial that tests graces and purifies character must be something more than a pin-scratch. It must cut deep, it must *try* us; and sharply too, or it does not deserve the name. It is hard to be poor while others prosper; it is hard to lie still and suffer while godless mirth goes laughing by the door; it is hard to lose our only wee lamb while our neighbour's fireside is surrounded by a group of rosy-cheeked children; it is hard to drink the very cup that we prayed might pass from us; but the loving shepherd comes very near at such times, and puts his arm about us and says: 'I know mine own, and mine own trust me. If mine, then an heir to all I have. Where I am, there you shall be; let not your heart be troubled. What is poverty, or failure, or sickness, or bereavement to you? *Follow me*. If your feet are sore, the green pastures will be all the softer by and by. If your cross is heavy, I have borne a heavier one. Let me share this with you. Shall the disciple be above his Master? Shall the sheep fare better than the Shepherd?'

And so through every step in life the Shepherd offers to

guide us, if we will but hear his voice and follow him. He never promises us smooth paths, but he does promise safe ones. When we obey his voice, we may often be called to severe toils and self-denials, to encounter opposition and to perform services of love to the unlovable and the thankless; but we shall never be called to sacrifice a principle or commit a sin. Our Shepherd will never lead us to a precipice of error or into a quagmire of doubt. He will never lead us into sensual temptations or up dizzy heights of vain-glory. If we follow him we may find the steepest cliff a 'path of pleasantness' and the lowest vale of humiliation a highway to peace. Brethren of the flock, we may have some hard climbing yet before we reach heaven. Let us keep close to the Shepherd and take short views. If we look down, we may get dizzy; if we look too far on, we may get discouraged. With steady grasp on the great Shepherd, let our hearts continually pray:

> Keep Thou my feet; I do not ask to see
> The distant scene; one step's enough for me.

# 10

# THE EVERLASTING ARMS

One of the sweetest passages in the Bible is this one: 'Underneath are the everlasting arms.' It is not often preached from; perhaps because it is felt to be so much richer and more touching than anything we ministers can say about it. But what a vivid idea it gives of the divine support! The first idea of infancy is of resting in arms which maternal love never allows to become weary. Sick-room experiences confirm the impression when we have seen a feeble mother or sister lifted from the bed of pain by the stronger ones of the household. In the case of our heavenly Father, the arms are felt, but not seen. The invisible secret support comes to the soul in its hours of weakness or trouble; for God knows our feebleness, he remembers that we are dust.

We often sink very low under the weight of sorrows. Sudden disappointments can carry us, in an hour, from the heights down to the very depths. Props that we leaned upon are stricken away. What God means by it very often is just to bring us down to 'the everlasting arms'. We did not feel our need of them before. We were 'making flesh our arm', and relying on human comforts or resources. When my little boy dashes off to his play, brimful of glee, he does not stop to think much about his parents; but let him be taken suddenly sick, or an accident befall him, his first thought is to go to his mother. God often lays his hand heavily upon us to remind us that we have a *Father*. When my neighbour A— broke in business, and twenty-four hours made him a bankrupt, he came home, saying to himself, 'Well, my money is gone, but Jesus is left.' He did not merely come down to 'hard pan', he came to something far more solid—to the everlasting arms. When another friend laid her beautiful boy in his coffin, after the scarlet-fever had done its worst, she laid her own sorrowful heart upon the everlasting arms. The dear little sleeper was there already. The Shepherd had his lamb.

There is something about deep sorrow that tends to wake up the *child*-feeling in all of us. A man of giant intellect becomes like a little child when a great grief smites him, or when a grave opens beneath his bedroom or his fireside. I have seen a stout sailor, who laughed at the tempest, come home when he was sick, and let his old mother nurse him as if he were a baby. He was willing to lean on the arms that had never failed him. So a Christian in the time of trouble is brought to this child-feeling. He wants to lean somewhere, to talk to somebody, to have somebody love him and hold him up. His extremity becomes God's opportunity. Then his humbled, broken spirit cries out:

> O Lord, a little helpless child
> Comes to Thee this day for rest
> Take me, fold me in Thy arms,
> Hold my head upon Thy breast.

One great purpose in all affliction is to bring us down to the everlasting arms. What new strength and peace it gives us to feel them underneath us! We know that, far as we may have sunk, we cannot go any farther. Those mighty arms can not only hold us, they can lift us up. They can carry us along. Faith, in its essence, is simply a resting on the everlasting arms. It is trusting them, and not our own weakness. The sublime act of Jesus as our Redeemer was to descend to the lowest depths of human depravity and guilt, and to bring up his redeemed ones from that horrible pit in his loving arms. Faith is just the clinging to those arms, and nothing more.

This first lesson in conversion is to be practised and repeated all through the subsequent Christian life. To endeavour to lift our own souls by our own strength is as absurd as to attempt to lift our bodies by grasping hold of our own clothes. The lift must come from God. Faith cries out, 'O my Lord, you have a mighty arm; hold me up.' The response from heaven is, 'I have found you; mine arm shall strengthen you; on my arm shall you trust.'

Here lies the very core of the doctrine of 'Assurance'. It simply means that I can feel, and every Christian believer can feel, perfectly sure that the everlasting arms will never break and never fail us. I am *not* so sure that in some moment of waywardness, or pride, or self-sufficiency, I may not forsake those arms, and trust to my own wretched weakness. Then the curse which God has pronounced on those who depart from him and 'make flesh their arm' is certain to come upon me. I learn from bitter experience what a pitiable object even a Christian can be when he has forsaken the living fountain, and has nothing left but his own broken cistern. God's Word is full of precious encouragement to faith, but it contains terrible warnings against presumption and self-confidence. And while Presumption is swinging on its spider's web over the perilous precipice, Faith calmly says:

> All my trust on Thee is stayed,
> All my help from Thee I bring.

While Unbelief is floundering through the darkness, or sinking in the waves of despair, Faith triumphantly sings:

> Safe in the arms of Jesus,
> Safe on his gentle breast,
> Here, by his love o'ershadowed,
> Sweetly my soul doth rest.

This is the theology for times of temptation. Such times are sure to come. They are the testing processes. A late Sunday's equinoctial gale tested every tree in the forest; only the rotten ones came down. When we read or hear how some professed Christian has turned defaulter, or lapsed into drunkenness, or slipped from the Communion table into open disgrace, it simply means that a human arm has broken. The man had forsaken the everlasting arms. David did it once, and fell. Daniel did not do it, and he stood. 'The Lord knoweth how to deliver *the godly* out of temptations.'

This is a precious theology, this theology of trust, for the sick-room. We called in this week to visit one of Christ's suffering flock. We talked for a time about the ordinary consolations for such cases as hers. Presently we said, 'There is a sweet text that has been running in our mind for days past: it is this—"Underneath are the everlasting arms."' The tears came in a moment; that precious passage went to the right spot; it did good like a medicine; and our suffering friend lay more comfortable on that bed of pain from feeling that underneath her were the everlasting arms. Reader, may they be under your head in the dying hour!

## 11

## WORDS FOR THE WEARY

Opening into one of those rich chapters of Isaiah, that are as full of nourishment as a wheat-field, our eye lighted upon this passage: 'The Lord God hath given me the tongue of the learned, that I should know how to speak a word in season to him that is weary.' This set us to thinking about the *restfulness* of God's Word and of Christ's supporting grace. A very different thing is this from dreamy indolence. God abhors the idle man as a monster, and laziness as a cardinal sin. But rest is not only refreshing, but invigorating. The farmer's noonday hour under the shady tree refits him for the hot afternoon's toil in the harvest-field. Nothing fits an army for battle like a good night's sleep and a full morning meal. If some 'terrible toilers' would oftener halt and rest, they would live the longer.

All around us are multitudes of weary people. They are tired out with life's daily battle, with bearing the heat and burden of the day. Some carry a great load of care as to how they shall make both ends meet, and how they shall 'foot' the bills for rent, food and clothes. Others are worn out with anxieties. A burden of spiritual despondency weighs down 'Brother Little-Faith' and 'Mrs Much-Afraid'. Another one has grown tired of waiting for success in his labours, and is tempted to throw down his seed-bag and sickle in sheer despair. Others still are weary of waiting for recognised answers to prayer.

For all these tired and burdened hearts Jesus, the relief-bringer, has his word in season. To the Christian with a small purse, he says: 'Your life consisteth not in the abundance of things ye possess. I counsel thee to buy of me gold tried in the fire, that thou mayest be rich. At my right hand are treasures for evermore.' Only think how rich a man is who has a clean conscience here and heaven hereafter! To the doubting and desponding Jesus says: 'Fear not, little flock; for it is my Father's good pleasure to give you the kingdom.' There is a wonderful restfulness for worried hearts in this single assurance, 'Lo, I am with you alway.' This may be called Christ's richest and sweetest promise. The believer who lives on that promise can often sing:

> I am never lonely
> While Jesus standeth by
> His presence always cheers me,
> I know that he is nigh.

Friendless? No, not friendless,
For Jesus is my friend;
I change, but he remaineth
A brother to the end.

Tired? No, not tired;
While leaning on his breast,
My soul hath full enjoyment
Of his eternal rest.

The most common cause of weariness is the attempt to carry an overload of care. And this is not a wise forethought for the future or a proper providence for life's 'rainy day'. It is sheer worry. The word in season for such overloaded Christians, who toil along life's highway like jaded pack-horses, is this: 'Cast thy burden on the Lord, and he shall sustain thee.' If we will only drop everything that is sinful and superfluous in the shape of worry, he will enable us to carry the legitimate load. One more word for the weary is, 'Cast your care on *him,* for he careth for you.' The literal meaning of this tonic text is: he has you on his heart. What an inspiring, gladdening thought! The infinite God from his everlasting throne has poor little sinful me on his divine heart! My big load is not a feather to him. He knows my frame; he remembers that I am dust. Like as a father pities his children, so the Lord pities us poor weaklings. He says to us, 'Give me your burdens.' He who piloted Noah and all the precious freight in the ark, who supplied the widow's waning cruse of oil, who put Peter to sleep in the dungeon and calmed Paul in the roaring tempest—he says to me, 'Roll your anxieties over on me. I have you on my heart.' What fools we are when we strap the load more tightly, and determine that nobody shall carry it but ourselves!

Suppose that a weary, foot-sore traveller were trudging along an up-hill road on a sultry day, and a wagon overtakes him. The kind driver calls out: 'Ho! my friend, you look tired. Throw that pack into my wagon; I am going your way.' But the silly wayfarer, eyeing him suspiciously, as if he wished to steal it, churlishly replies, 'Go along with you. I can carry my own luggage.' We laugh at this obstinate folly, and then repeat the same insane sin against the God of love.

When God says to us, 'Give me your load, and I will help you', he does not release us from our share of duty. No more does the atoning Saviour when he bears the guilt and penalty of our sins, release us from repentance of those sins or from obeying his commandments. God's offer is to lighten our loads by putting his grace into our hearts and underneath the load. He then becomes our strength. His all-sufficient grace is made perfect in our weakness, so that God really carries the load. It was the Christ *in* Paul who defied Nero and conquered the devil.

This divine doctrine of trust is a wonderfully restful one to weary disciples. It takes the tiredness out of the heart. As the infant drops over on mother's bosom into soft repose, so Faith rests its weary head on Jesus. He gives his beloved sleep, so that they may wake up refreshed for their appointed work.

It is not honest work that really wears any Christian out. It is the ague-fit of worry that consumes strength and furrows the cheek and brings on decrepitude. That giant of Jesus Christ who drew the gospel chariot from Jerusalem to Rome, and had the care of all the churches on his great heart, never complained of being tired. The secret was that he never chafed his powers with a moment's worry. He was doing God's work, and he left God to be responsible for results. He knew whom he believed, and felt perfectly sure that all things work together for good to them who love the Lord Jesus.

Just a word, in closing, to those who are getting tired of a life of sin and of serving Satan. Friends, you are serving a hard master. His wages are death. Again and again you have become disgusted with yourselves as leading a frivolous, foolish life for an immortal being. All the pleasures you have ever paid so dearly for, all the accumulations you have earned, do not satisfy you. There is a hungry, aching spot in your soul. There comes many a moment in which you wish you had something solider, sweeter, stronger, something to live for and to die by. You need Jesus Christ! Wherefore do you spend your labour for that which does not satisfy? Open your weary ear to that voice of his love: 'Come unto me, all ye that labour and are heavy laden, and I will give you rest.' Learn of him; live for him; labour for him. Life will glow with a new charm; your soul will then mount as with an eagle's wing; you will run, and never weary, you will walk with Jesus, and never faint.

## 12

## THE LORD REIGNS

What a magnificent outburst of loyalty opens the ninety-third psalm! 'The Lord reigneth, he is clothed with majesty; the Lord is clothed with strength, wherewith he hath girded himself. Thy throne is established of old: thou art from everlasting.' Here we have the empire of love, the royal robe, the girdle of omnipotence, and the immovable throne. The psalmist would seem to have been thinking of the problems of life, its dark things and its mysteries. So many things seemed irreconcilable with the divine goodness that he admits that 'clouds and darkness are round about him.' But this truth flashes out through the clouds—*the Lord reigns*. That is enough. He does not try to pry into the council-chamber. He cannot get behind the cloud. But love reigns there, and justice and righteousness are the foundations of that throne.

Not one of us has any trouble in accepting this doctrine of God's sovereignty as long as things go to our liking. We are perfectly satisfied to let God have his way as long as he does not cross us. We all believe in his administration, and are ready (as Dr Finney used to say) to 'vote God in as our governor' as long as business thrives, and crops are plentiful, and everyone around our own table is hearty and happy. As long as his mercies are poured out in wine, we drink of them gladly; but as soon as the same cup begins to taste of wormwood, we push it away in disgust, or cry out piteously, 'Let this cup pass from me.' Any other cup we could have swallowed, but not this one. If God had only tried us with the loss of our property, and spared us our health, we could have borne it; or if he had sent the sickness at some other time, we would not murmur so; or if his blow had struck us somewhere else but in our very tenderest spot, we should not cry out so bitterly. In short, if God had only consulted us as to the medicine we should take, and as to the branch his pruning knife should lop off, we would have been perfectly submissive. Every pastor encounters this kind of faith in God's sovereignty wherever he goes. If the Lord governed so as to please everybody, there would not be a rebel in all his universe.

As some of our readers may just now be smarting under God's strokes of discipline, or letting their hearts fester into rebellion, let us whisper a few truths into their ears. The first is that our heavenly Father never afflicts one of his children but for a wise purpose. He never strikes at random, or deals one blow in cruelty. Sometimes his chastisements are *punitive*. Christians deserve punishment as truly as ungodly blasphemers do when they violate God's laws. A lazy Christian will come to want as soon as a lazy profligate. If as holy a man as Dr Payson breaks some of God's sanitary regulations by overworking his nervous system, and allowing himself no recreations, he must expect shattered nerves and early paralysis.[1] One of the excellences of God's government is that he never alters his laws to suit special cases. They are unchangeable. And I have heard of a great many 'mysterious providences' that had in them no mystery at all. They were simply righteous retributions. There is no mystery when a bad manager, even though he be a Christian, fails in business, or when a Christian merchant that has robbed himself of indispensable rest is stricken with softening of the brain. A thousand so-called 'providences' might have been prevented by the exercise of a little common sense and conscience. If we break God's commandments, we must pay the penalty.

[1] Edward Payson (1783-1827), minister of the Second (Congregational) Church in Portland, Maine, from 1807 until his relatively early death from tuberculosis. His biographer, Asa Cummings, comments: 'It is almost incredible, what abstinence and self-denial he voluntarily underwent, and what tasks he imposed on himself, that he might "bring every thought into captivity to the obedience of Christ." He allowed himself only a small part of the twenty-four hours for sleep; and his seasons for fasting were injuriously frequent. So far did he carry his abstinence from food, that his family were alarmed for his safety.' (*A Memoir of Rev Edward Payson, DD* [London: Seeley & Burnside, 2nd English Edition, 1832], p. 60.) Payson was the father of the author Elizabeth Prentiss – see Sharon James, *Elizabeth Prentiss—More Love to Thee* (Edinburgh: Banner of Truth, 2006). *Ed.*

Sometimes our sovereign sends afflictions that are *preventive*. They save us from something worse. As the headache and the self-loathing that follow a first bottle are intended to warn us against touching another, so God often puts a chastisement at the entrance to a path of danger. There is even a conserving influence in some severe trials, just as the early snows that are now falling on our northern hills will conserve the winter wheat. I can recall more than one chilling providence which came in time to keep me from losing what I could not afford to spare.

Still other afflictions are sent to *purify* character. God sits as a refiner beside his furnace. He heats it until the metal melts and the dross runs away. He keeps his silver in the furnace until he can see his own face reflected in the clear metal of the heart as in a mirror. Then the affliction has done its work. God has made the vessel 'unto his own honour'. There is such a wretched amount of self-will and pride and covetousness and unbelief even in undoubted Christians, that they require the fining-pot very often. Many a man and woman has been the worse for want of this kind of discipline.

It is a wholesome process to be 'taken down' occasionally. The grass in every lawn requires to be taken down by a mower. The oftener it is mowed the richer and the thicker is the growth. The lawn never looks so beautiful as after the keen-edged cutter has gone over it. I have observed that some Christians in my charge have never appeared so attractive in their humility and heavenly-mindedness as when God's mowing-machine has been passed over them. The great apostle's career, as I read it in the masterly consecutive narrative of Canon Farrar, showed in almost every page the effects of the scythe. There was prodigious growth from the roots. Yet no man exalted God's sovereignty more heartily than Paul. He gloried even in the tribulations which God permitted him to suffer, knowing that tribulation works patience, and patience experience, and experience hope. This too he knew, that in all this process the love of God was shed abroad in his heart by the Holy Ghost given unto him.

We have discussed in this short chapter just one aspect of God's government, namely, his personal rule of our own personal lives and lot. His sovereignty on the grander scale of the natural world, and of his vast spiritual kingdom we leave out of sight. It is a blessed thought that the Lord reigns over little short-lived me as truly as over the whole church or the whole universe. He numbers the hairs of my head, and orders my steps. Let it be my daily and devoutest aim to lay the plan of my life on God's plan. If his immovable laws push me back and hedge me in from sin, then all the better. If his sharp knife prunes me, then I am only the more sure that he loves me. Afflictions are like the cactus plant of his making, very unsightly and full of thorns, but they bear marvellous flowers in their time.

God's government is the solidest ground of my confidence and joy. It underlies all my theology, and is the very rock-bed on which I rest my salvation. While Jehovah reigns, let me rejoice to obey him. To oppose him is to invite his retributions, and that means—hell! To submit to him is to win his favour, and to secure his love, and that means—heaven! The nearer we get to the throne the more loudly shall we sing, 'The Lord God omnipotent reigneth!'

## 13

## Up to the Hills

*T*he one hundred and twenty-first psalm is one of the most soul-inspiring in the whole Psalter. It is named 'A Song of Degrees'; that is, a Song of Ascents, leading from the lower up to the higher. Whether this was originally intended as a musical expression or as a description of the ascent to the sacred mount in Jerusalem, it happily describes the spiritual idea of the psalm. The key-note is in the first verse: 'I will lift up mine eyes unto the hills [or mountains] from whence cometh my help. My help is from the Lord, which made heaven and earth.' The grand idea is that we must look higher if we would live higher. We must have help from heaven if we would reach heaven.

In things material and in things spiritual not one of us is created to entire independence. From infancy, when we depend on a mother's milk for nourishment, and childhood, when we depend on our teachers for instruction, clear through the activities of manhood, which require the aid of customers and clients in order to prosper, we cannot ever live a year in and by ourselves. Still more true is it that our moral life is one of weakness and of want. The important question is: *Where* shall we find the supplies for the soul's wants and the help for the soul's weakness? And the fatal mistake so often made is that the soul does not look high enough to secure substantial help and to insure a complete victory. For example, we are exposed to perpetual temptations, which draw us toward sin and thus tend to drag us downward. How are we to meet them?

We may employ arguments that are wholly of the earth, earthy. They have no motives that are not essentially selfish; they do not recognise anything higher than self-interest, or appeal to any supernatural power for aid. Here is a young man of ardent temperament, who is strongly tempted to sensual indulgence. He may say to himself: 'This will not pay for the risks. I shall injure my health; I shall stain the reputation of another; I may be discovered and disgraced.' Assuredly the young Hebrew who was put to the strain of a tremendous temptation in the house of Potiphar laid hold of vastly higher motives than these. He lifted his eyes to the hills and made his appeal to God. 'How can I do this great wickedness', he cries out, 'and sin against God?' That appeal lashed him, as it were, to the everlasting throne, and divine grace made him temptation-proof.

Here is the only safeguard under the pressure of assaults against conscience or of powerful enticements to some sinful self-gratification. The young man who is too fond of the champagne-glass needs something more than the conviction that the bottle is endangering his health and his pocket in order to keep him abstinent. He must recognise *sin,* as well as sorrow, in the sting which the 'viper in the glass' inflicts, and seek his help from the highest. That is no trustworthy honesty which spurns the enticement to fraud simply because detection may bring disgrace, because the man may persuade himself that in his circumstances detection is impossible. He is only safe when he looks up from these paltry motives—up high enough to *see* God. In these days, when the press teems with obituaries of lost characters, it ought to be known that the only principle which can hold a merchant, or a cashier, or an accountant, is a Bible-conscience, which draws its strength from the everlasting hills of right.

There are some of us who have known what it is to drink bitter draughts of affliction, and to have the four corners of our house smitten by a terrible sorrow. At such times, how hollow and worthless were many of the stereotyped prescriptions for comfort! 'Time must do its work', was one of them. As if time could bring back the dead, or cruelly eradicate the beloved image from the memory! 'Travel', is another of these quack recommendations for a wounded spirit. Just as if God had ever made an Atlantic wide enough to carry us out of the reach of heartbreaking misery! Wretched comforters are they all. The suffering heart heeds not the voice of such charmers, charm they never so wisely. Never, never have I been able to gain one ray of genuine consolation until I lifted my eyes unto the hills from whence comes the almighty help. As soon as I have begun to taste of God's exceeding great and precious promises my strength has begun to revive. As soon as his everlasting arm got hold around me the burden grew lighter—yea, it carried me and the load likewise. God opened to me paths of usefulness which were in the line of his service, and also of blessings to my fellow-men. And so help flowed down to me from the hills like the streams that make music from the precipices to one who climbs the Wenzern Alp.

This sublime passage from the hundred and twenty-first psalm throws its suggestive sidelight on the question why many of my readers have never obtained a solid and satisfactory religious hope. You will admit in your honest hours that you are not what you ought to be, nor what you yet intend to be. You admit that you are sinners. You have no expectation of being lost to all eternity. Certain steps you have taken in past times, but they all left you as low down as you started. Both your motives and your methods were pitched too low. All attempts at self-salvation were as futile as would be the attempt to lift yourself by grasping hold of your own shoes. Even relig-

ious services failed to bring you any substantial change
of heart and character, because you did not get your eye
or thought above them. The best sermon ever preached is
only a cup, after all. It may bring the water, but the cup
itself cannot quench thirst.

What you need is to lift your eyes above your sinful,
needy self, above your church-goings and other religious
observances, above everyone and everything, to the only
mountain whence comes your help. That mountain is
Calvary. The crucified and now living Son of God is
the object on which you must fix your eye. As a living
man, you need a living Christ. You want not a system
of doctrine, but a personal Saviour. You need someone
not only to lay your hand upon, but one who can return
the grasp of that hand. The lift must come from him.
The new life must come from him. 'His blood cleanseth
from all sin' is a mere abstract truth until you come up to
that atoning blood for yourself. Submit to its cleansing,
as Naaman submitted to be washed in Jordan. 'A living
trust in Jesus has power unto salvation only because it is
the means by which the saving power of God may come
into your heart.' Faith is not a mere intellectual opinion.
It is a heart transaction, by which you lay hold on Jesus,
and Jesus saves. His sacrifice for sin avails for you; his
strength becomes yours; his example teaches you how to
live your own daily life; his Spirit comes to dwell within
you; his armour protects you; and his service becomes the

[73]

inspiration of your whole being. When you ascend into Christ you reach a loftier, purer atmosphere. Security is gained up there as in a stronghold on a cliff. Six times over in this psalm the inspired penman tells us how the Lord is your keeper, and how he shall preserve your soul to all eternity. My friend, lift your eyes upward. Let your voice go up in fervent prayer to the everlasting hills. Put your feet firmly on the path that leads straight toward God. When you reach him in this world you have reached heaven in the next world.

# 14

## RIGHT SEEING

'Thou hast well seen.' These were God's words to Jeremiah when he called him to his life-work as a 'seer' or prophet to the people of Israel. He puts to the modest, self-distrustful young man the question, 'What seest thou?' Jeremiah replies, 'I see a rod of an almond tree.' This is just what the Lord meant that he should see; the almond was a tree of rapid growth and early bloom; it typified speedy action. As the young Jew had shown his capacity for right discernment, the Lord commended his wise answer, and said to him, 'Thou hast well seen.'

There is a right way and a wrong way of looking at almost everything. To a man who has no eye for beauty, one of Claude's landscapes is merely so much paint and linen canvas; to another it is a masterpiece of golden sunlight bathing field and forest with its glory.[1] To many it

[1] Claude Gellé, (c. 1604-82) was a French-born artist who used Italian landscapes combined with classical features, e.g., 'Landscape with David at the Cave of Adullam', 1658. *Ed.*

was predicted that Christ, the Messiah, would be as 'a root out of dry ground, having no form or comeliness. When they shall see him, there is no beauty that they should desire him; he will be despised and rejected of men.' When he came, therefore, to his own, they received him not. As many as beheld him rightly and received him, to them gave he the privilege of becoming the children of God. He is to them the chief among ten thousand, and the altogether lovely. Christ never changes. The difference between the thoughtless sinner and the same person after he is converted is that he looks at him with a new eye, and sees him to be the very Saviour that he needs.

Some people look at God only as a consuming fire, and are struck with despair. Others go to the opposite extreme, and see in him nothing but pity and pardoning mercy; they easily slide off into Universalism. But the man who magnifies God's mercy at the expense of his justice, and who does not believe that he will punish sin as it deserves, has not 'well seen'. He will be cured of his delusion on the day of judgment. Those wise men at Westminster saw the divine being, our heavenly Father, in the right proportions of his attributes when they framed that wonderful answer to that question in the Catechism, 'What is God?'

In nothing are we all apt to make more terrible blunders than in looking at God's providential dealings. Even some Christians have a heathenish habit of talking about 'good luck' and 'windfalls' and 'bad fortune', and other expressions that convey the idea that this life is a mere game of chance. Blind unbelief may be expected to err, and to scan God's work as either a riddle or a muddle. A Christian, who has had his eyes opened, ought to know better. Yet how often do we all regard God's dealings in a wrong light, and call them by the wrong name! We frequently speak of certain things as afflictions when they are really blessings in disguise. We congratulate people on gaining what turns out to be a terrible snare or a worse than loss. Quite as often we condole with them over a lot which is about to yield to them mercies more precious than gold. Old Jacob probably thought that he was a fair subject for commiseration on that evening when he sat moaning in his tent-door; but the caravan was just approaching which brought him Simeon and Benjamin, and glorious tidings about the long-lost Joseph. He had not well seen what sort of a God he was serving.

Let us hesitate before we condole with a brother who is under the chastisement of our loving Father in heaven. Be careful how you condole with a man who has lost his money and saved his good name, or congratulate the man who has made a million at the expense of his piety. When a Christian is toppled over from a dizzy and dangerous height, and 'brought down to hard pan', he is brought down to the solid rock at the same time. In the valley of humiliation he has more of the joy of God's countenance, and wears more of the herb called 'heart's-ease' in his bosom, than he ever did in the days of his giddy prosperity. Sickness has often brought to a man spiritual recovery; suffering has often wrought out for him an exceeding weight of glory. The writer of this paragraph has lately been led through a very shadowy pathway of trial;[2] but it has never been so dark that he could not see to read some precious promises that glowed like diamonds. The adversary tries hard to break our lamp, and to steal our diamonds in those dark passage-ways of trial. We need good eyesight in such times of trouble, so as not to stumble, or to lose sight of the Comforter, or of the bright light which shines at the end of the way.

I have seen people condole tenderly with a weeping mother whose child has flown away home to heaven; but they never thought of condoling with her over a living child who was a frivolous slave of fashion, or a dissipated sensualist, or a wayward son, the 'heaviness of his mother.' A hundred times over have I pitied more the parent of a living sorrow than the parent of a departed joy. Spare your tears from the darlings who are safe in the arms of Jesus, and spend them over the living who are yet dead in sin and sheer impenitence. Let us learn to see things rightly, and call them by their right names. We too often drape our real blessings with a pall, and decorate our dangerous

---

[2] See NOTE at the end of this book which referes to the death of Cuyler's twenty-two year old daughter, Louise. *Ed.*

temptations with garlands. The sharpest trials this nation ever knew have turned into tender mercies. Garfield in his grave has done more for us than Garfield could have done in the presidential chair. Satan outwitted himself when he armed one of his imps to be an assassin.[3]

Let us all pray fervently for spiritual discernment. Lord, open our eyes! Then we shall see this world to be a mere training-school for a better world; we shall see a Father's smile behind the darkest cloud; we shall see in duty done our highest delight; and at the end of the conflict we shall *see the King in his beauty,* and know him even as we are known.

---

[3] See the note in the second paragraph of the first chapter—'God's Light on Dark Clouds' pp. 2-3. *Ed.*

## 15

## THE LORD OUR STRENGH

*T*he first lesson of childhood is human weakness. The
earliest cry of the infant betrays it. At the other end
of life we often see a pitiable dotage, such as I encountered lately in the case of a man who was once a luminary
of the American pulpit, but now cannot remember the
names of his own children. But the weakest side of humanity is its moral side. Colossal intellect is often found
lodged in the same person with a conscience of mere pulp.
For the sake of morality, I rejoice that Madame de Rémusat and Metternich have lately been stripping away
the glamour that has hung around that stupendous em-
bodiment of selfishness, Napoleon I.[1] They show us the
intellectual giant continually pushed over with a straw.

[1] *The Memoirs of Madame de Rémusat* were first published in English in
1880. Claire Élisabeth Jeanne Gravier de Vergennes de Rémusat (1780-1821)
was a lady-in-waiting, friend and confidant to the Empress Josephine. *The
Memoirs of Prince Metternich* were published in English in three volumes
between 1880 and 1882. Clemens Fürst von Metternich (1773-1859) was an
Austrian statesman and diplomat in post-Napoleonic Europe. *Ed.*

The chief lesson of such a career as Napoleon's is to demonstrate what a contemptible creature man is the moment he cuts loose from God.

One of the chief purposes of our divine religion is to teach man where to find this indispensable element of *strength*. The divine Word, coming from the very Maker of man, who knows us completely, declares that 'he who trusteth in his own heart is a fool.' We have no spiritual strength in ourselves. Just as our bodies derive all their strength from the food we eat, and every oak draws its strength from the surrounding earth and air, so our souls obtain all spiritual power from a source outside of us. Psalmist David, whose native weaknesses were deplorably conspicuous, was only strong when in alliance with God. His declaration is, 'The Lord is my strength.' This is the only strength which the Bible recognises. Who are the Bible heroes? Men of genius, wits, orators, philosophers? No. They are the Enoch who walked with God, the Joseph who conquered sensual temptation because God was with him, the Elijah who stood like a granite pillar against the tides of idolatry, and the Daniel who never quailed at the lion's roar. Daniel gives us the secret of his strength in his three-times-a-day interviews with God. The Lord fed his inner soul as the subterranean springs feed a well and keep it full during summer droughts.

God's strength is 'made perfect in our weakness'. This means that the divine power is most conspicuous when our weakness is the most thoroughly felt. We have got first to be emptied of all self-conceit and self-confidence. A bucket cannot hold air and water at the same time. As the water comes in the air must go out. The meaning of some hard trials is to get the accursed spirit of self out of our hearts. When we have been emptied of self-trust, we are in the condition to be filled with might in the inner man by the power of the Holy Spirit. When Isaiah felt that he was but a child, and an unclean one at that, he received the touch of celestial fire. Peter had immense confidence in Peter when he boasted of his own strength; but after pride had got its fall, Peter is endued with power from on high, and then the apostle who was frightened by a servant-girl could face a Sanhedrin. A Christian must not only realize his own utter feebleness, but he must give up what worldlings rely on, and admit that 'vain is the help of man.'

That poor woman who had tried all the doctors in her neighbourhood, and had only grown worse in body and poorer in purse, is a touching illustration of our invalid souls. She despaired of human help, and came crouching to the feet of the Son of God. One touch of his garments sent a new tide of health through her veins. Contact with Christ brings currents of the divine power into our souls, so that we can do all things through Christ who strengthens us. At the very outset of the spiritual life this divine strength becomes recognised. A Gough or a Sawyer testifies that he gained his victory over the bottle by the influx of a new principle and a new power into his heart.[2] The essence of conversion with them was that the seven devils of lust for the cup were cast out, and Christ came in. This was a supernatural work, the very thing that modern scepticism hoots at; but a Bible which did not bring a supernatural element into weak and wicked humanity would not be worth the paper on which it is printed. If the Christ of Christianity cannot and does not endow a frail sinner with supernatural power to resist terrible temptations, then is Christianity a confessed im-

[2] John B. Gough (1817-86). Born in Sandgate, Kent, England, Gough emigrated to the United States aged twelve with his mother and sister. His mother died of a stroke and Gough, despondent, began to drink. He married in 1838. The couple had a daughter but tragically, both mother and child died within days of each other. By the age of 25, Gough was unemployed, homeless, and a confirmed drunkard. In 1842 he attended a temperance meeting in Worcester, Massachusetts, where he took a pledge to abstain totally from liquor. He began to tell his story to eager audiences and soon embarked on a career of lecturing against the evils of drink. During his career, Gough delivered some 9,600 lectures to more than 9 million people in America, Canada, England, Scotland, and Ireland. When he died in 1886, the *New York Times* wrote that he 'was probably better known in this country and in Great Britain than any other public speaker'. He was a witnessing Christian, a personal friend of Spurgeon, and shared the pulpit in Boston (1877) during a 'Temperance Day' meeting with D. L. Moody. According to a report in the *New York Times,* C. F. Sawyer was an evangelist who held 'Gospel Temperance Meetings' at Cooper Union in New York around the time Cuyler was writing. These meetings were 'song services' with large choirs and frequently Ira D. Sankey as soloist. Testimonies by converted drunkards were given before Sawyer and/or others—including Moody—preached the gospel. Sawyer is mentioned as a co-worker of D. L. Moody in *Moody: His Words, Work and Workers* (New York: Nelson and Phillips, 1877).] *Ed.*

posture and delusion. But it does stand this very crucial test. Multitudes have given the triumphant testimony that, under sore pressure, the Lord stood with them and strengthened them. Their testimony has always been, 'When I am weak, then am I strong'—that is, when I get emptied of self-trust, Jesus comes in and strengthens me. Charles G. Finney has left us some wonderful experiences of the prodigious tides of power which poured into his soul and into his work when he humbled himself before God, and put his own soul, like an empty vessel, under the divine power, until he became filled 'unto all the fulness of God'.

This is the real office of faith. It is simply the linking of our utter weakness to the omnipotence of Christ. We furnish weakness and he furnishes strength, and that makes the partnership. The baby furnishes a hungry little mouth, and the mother furnishes the nourishing milk. The mother is happy that she can give the full supply, and the rosy darling is happy as it draws in the sweet contentment. Beautiful picture of my poor, weak, hungry soul resting on the bosom of the infinite love! There is no danger that the supply will ever give out, for my Lord, my feeder, my supporter, is constantly saying unto me, 'My grace is sufficient for thee.' In this way we are strengthened with all might according to his glorious power. A happier translation of the sentence in Colossians 1 would be, '*in*forced with all force'. We have retained the word 'reinforce' in the English language, and it is a pity that we have dropped the older word 'inforce', for it describes exactly the impartation of the divine strength to a believer's soul.

Alas, how easily we run dry, and how constantly we need replenishment! Yesterday's breakfast will not feed me tomorrow. The Christian who tried to live on the experiences of last year were as insane as if he attempted to work on the food eaten a month ago. Lord, *evermore* give us this bread! They that wait on the Lord shall renew their strength, the waste shall constantly be repaired, and the new emergency shall be met with a fresh supply.

One great purpose in all afflictions is to bring us down to the everlasting arms. We had become presumptuous, and had made flesh our arm. We were trying to go alone, and then came a fall. Trouble, and even bereavement, may be a great blessing, if it sends us home to Jesus. A boy often forgets that he has a home until a cut or a bruise sends him crying to his mother's side for the bandage or the medicine. God often strikes away our props to bring us down upon his mighty arms. What strength and peace it gives us to feel them underneath us! Far as we may sink, we cannot go farther down than those outstretched arms. There we stop, there we rest; and the everlasting arms not only sustain us, but carry us along, as on eagles' wings. Faith is just the clinging of my weak soul to the omnipotent Jesus; its constant cry is:

I am weak, but Thou art mighty:
Hold me with thy powerful hand.

To that hand let me cling with all the five fingers of my faith. It will never let me drop until it lands me in glory.

## 16

## A Constant Salvation

*A* clipper ship crossing the Banks of Newfoundland in heavy weather strikes an iceberg. She settles rapidly at the bow, and her captain and crew have barely time to leap into the life-boat. The question, 'What must we do to be saved?' is answered by their prompt leap into the life-boat, which is an act of faith. They trust their lives to it for salvation. From immediate death they are saved.

But, after the ship has sunk, the crew are still out in the deep and dangerous sea. There is a second process necessary. In order to keep out of the trough of the sea and to reach the distant shore, they must stick to the boat and pull lustily at the oars. They must 'work out their salvation' now by hard rowing. But this is a *continued* process of salvation day after day until they reach the shores of Nova Scotia. Never for a moment, however, are they independent of the life-boat. That must keep them afloat, or they go to the bottom. At last, after hard rowing, they reach the welcome shore. This is their third, final, and complete salvation, for they are entirely beyond any perils of the treacherous sea. Now they are at rest, for they have reached the desired haven.

This homely parable will illustrate with sufficient clearness the three ways in which the word *salvation* is employed in God's Word and in human experience. The first leap into the lifeboat illustrates that decisive act of the soul in quitting all other worthless reliances and throwing itself on Christ Jesus in simple, believing trust. This is conversion. By it the soul is delivered from the guilt and condemnation of sin.

The Holy Spirit is active in this step, cleansing and renewing the heart. By this act of surrender to Christ the sinner escapes from death into life. He may joyfully cry out, 'By the grace of God I am *saved!*'

Yet this converted believer is no more independent of Christ as a Saviour than those sailors were of that lifeboat; for until he reaches the consummated deliverance of *heaven* (which is what the word 'salvation' signifies in *Psa.* 91:16) he must be clinging to Christ Jesus every day. And it is this daily and hourly salvation that we wish to emphasize at present. Too many people limit the word to the initial step of converting faith, and falsely conclude that nothing more is to be done. A certain school of rather mystical Christians so magnify this act of receiving the 'gift of eternal life' in Christ that they quite forget the fact that a vast deal of head winds, hard rowing, conflict with the devil and remaining lusts must be encountered.

There is a very important sense in which every true servant of Christ is obliged to 'work out his salvation' every day of his life, even if he lives a century. It was not to impenitent sinners or anxious inquirers that Paul addressed the famous in injunction, 'Work out your own salvation with fear and trembling'; he was addressing the blood-bought church at Philippi. And if he were alive to-day he might well ring these solemn words into the ears of every Christian in the land. For if our original deliverance from the condemnation of sin and from the desert of hell depended on our surrender to Christ, so our constant salvation from the assaults of sin depends upon our constant clinging to the Saviour and our constant *obedience* to his commandments. Faith without works is dead. Brethren, we may be in the life-boat, but the life-boat is not heaven. There is many a hard tug at the oar, many a night of tempest, many a danger from false lights, and many a scud under bare poles (with pride's 'top-hamper' all gone), before we reach the shining shore. To the last moment on earth our salvation depends on complete submission to Jesus. Without him, nothing; with him, all things.

Please bear in mind that salvation signifies simply the process of saving. Our blessed Master means to save us and our lives for himself, if we will let him do it and will honestly co-operate with him. Yonder is an acre of weeds which its owner wishes to save from barrenness to fruitfulness; so he subjugates it with plough and harrow and all the processes of cultivation. If the soil should cry out against the ploughshare and the harrow and the hoe, the farmer's answer would be, 'Only by submission to this discipline can I rear the golden crop which shall be to your credit and to my glory.' In like manner, by absolute submission to Christ's will, by constant obedience to his pure commandments, by the readiness to be used by him entirely for his own purposes can you or I be saved to life's highest end. The instant that I realize entirely that I am Christ's I must also realize that my time must be saved from waste for him and my influence must be consecrated to him. All accumulation is by wise saving. Sin means waste, and ends in ruin and remorse. The honest, devoted Christian is literally 'working out his salvation' when he is daily striving to redeem his time, and employ his utmost capacity, and use his every opportunity to make his life a beautiful offering and possession for his Lord. If we were not worth saving, our Lord would never have tasted the bitter agonies of Golgotha to redeem us. If every saved follower is by and by to be presented by Christ 'faultless, with exceeding joy', then is a Christian life a jewel worthy of his diadem. O my soul, let him work in me to will and to do according to his good pleasure, if I can be made to yield this revenue of honour to my beloved Lord!

There is another sense in which Christ furnishes us a constant salvation. His presence saves me in the hour of strong temptation. He keeps me from falling in a thousand cases where I do not directly recognise his hand. When I wake up in the morning, after a night ride in a Pullman car, I do not know how many human hands have been busy in order that I might ride safely through the pitch darkness; and when I get to heaven, perhaps I may find out how often Jesus interposed to save me from threatened ruin and from unsuspected dangers. He was saving me in a hundred ways that I did not dream of, and the visible acknowledged deliverances were all due to him. Daily grace means a daily salvation. Paul lived thus in constant dependence, realizing that if Christ withdrew his arm he must sink in an instant. Not for one moment can I dispense with the life-boat until my foot stands where 'there is no more sea'.

If these things be true, then we ought ever to be praying: 'O Lord, what must I *do* now to be saved? To be saved from waste of time; to be saved from dishonouring you; to be saved from secret sin; and to be saved up to the fullest, richest, holiest service of yourself?' He can help us to accomplish all this, for his grace can bring us a full salvation. When we reach heaven, we shall no longer need to be saved. The voyage will be over, the dangers ended; the multitudes who have been saved will then walk in the light of the new Jerusalem, and cast their crowns at the feet of him who purchased for us so ineffably glorious and transcendent a *salvation*.

## 17

## HEALTHY AND HAPPY

The Christmas bells are ringing in the brightest day in the Christian calendar. The clock of time will soon strike for the birth of another twelvemonth, when every man will wish his neighbour a 'Happy New Year!' To many it will no doubt be a day of sadness, for it will remind them of the loved ones whom the past year has buried out of their sight; but every genuine disciple of Jesus, every heir of heaven, ought to possess deep and abiding resources of joy, that lie as far beneath the tempests of trial as the depths of the Atlantic are beneath the storms that have lately torn its surface into foaming billows. Every healthy Christian ought to be a happy Christian under every stress of circumstances.

A living Christian who is worthy of the name must possess more or less of the *holiness* without which no man can see the Lord. There is a misconception and a prejudice in the minds of some good people in regard to this word, on account of the abuse of it by certain visionaries of the 'perfectionist' school. But holiness signifies health of heart and life. It is equivalent to the Saxon word *wholth,* and to be holy is really to be whole or healed. Sin is soul-sickness; regeneration by the divine Spirit is recovery from that sickness. There is no condemnation of guilt to them who are in Christ Jesus; he is the Physician who delivers them from deadly disease. If good health means misery, then is a sincere Christian a miserable mope; but if health means a happy condition, then should Christ's redeemed ones be the most cheerful, sunny-hearted people in the community.

There are several characteristics of a true child of God. One of them is that he is forgiven. To be pardoned has made many a prison-door like a gate of paradise. The sweet sense of sin forgiven has been an ecstasy to thousands who had 'groaned, being burdened', but had found relief at the cross of Christ. Another evidence of spiritual health is a good conscience—a conscience enlightened by the Bible, a conscience kept sweet and wholesome by prayer, a conscience that comforts its possessor, instead of tormenting him by a certain fearful looking-for of judgment. What a diseased liver is in the bodily organization, is a bad conscience in the spiritual man; it breeds continual mischief and misery. 'How is your liver?' was the first question of a shrewd and humorous old minister to me on my entrance into the ministry. When I told him that it was sound, he replied, 'Then *you'll do.'* The Christian never suffers from spiritual dyspepsia who keeps a conscience void of offence towards God and man.

A healthy soul has a strong appetite for divine truth. He enjoys the daily manna of the Word, and has no lustings for the 'fleshpots' of the world. It is not the stimulant of spiced pastry that he is after, but the strong meat of the gospel as well as the honeycomb. His soul 'delights itself in the fatness' of God's Word. To some people Mr Moody's style of talking about the banquet which the Bible affords him seems like extravagance; the reason is, that their spiritual taste is utterly corrupted by feeding on such confectionery as novels and secular newspapers. A combination of Bible-diet and Bible-duties would soon make them as vigorous as Mr Moody. If he did not show in his own conduct and condition the 'feeding' he lives on, he would not make many converts.

Holiness is constant agreement with God. It is the agreement of love—deeper even and sweeter than the most unbroken wedlock. From this harmony of soul with the divine will flows a great, deep, broad river of peace, which passes all understanding and fathoming. This stream grows deeper and wider, until, like an Amazon, it empties into the ocean of eternal love. The holy believer—who accepts God's promises more readily than the best government bonds, who shapes his life in conformity with Christ, who keeps his soul's windows open towards the sunrising, who makes even a cross the ladder for a climb into a higher fellowship with Jesus, who realizes that just before him lies the exceeding and eternal weight of glory — cannot be made a sour or peevish or melancholy man by any outward circumstances. The holy-minded Rutherford of Scotland wrote most of his immortal *Letters* within the cell of a martyr's prison. They read like leaves from the tree of life, floated down on sunbeams. 'Come, O my well-beloved!' he exclaims; 'move fast that we may meet at the banquet. I would not exchange one smile of Christ's lovely face for kingdoms. There is no house-room for crosses in heaven. Sorrow and the saints are not married together; or, if it were so, heaven would divorce them.'[1] The holiness of such a man is not the enthusiasm of a visionary or the mere outburst of transient emotion; it is the normal condition of the man, the *wholeness* of a soul that has been transformed by grace into the likeness and the life of Jesus Christ. Keeping Christ's command-ments keeps the eye clear and the temper sweet, and the will submissive, and the affections pure: in these lies the rich reward.

The highest type of piety is cheerful. The more we study the lives and examples of the healthiest Christians,

[1] Samuel Rutherford (1600-61), Scottish pastor, theologian, political theorist, and devotional writer. Quotations taken from three letters: Letter CLII, 14 March 1637 to Mr Thomas Garvan (p. 284); Letter XXIII, 13 February 1632 to Lady Kenmure (p. 78); Letter CCXLII, 7 September 1637 to Lady Rowallan (p. 479). The letter and page numbers are those in the Banner of Truth reprint of the 1891 edition of *Letters of Samuel Rutherford*, ed. Andrew Bonar, which includes an account of Rutherford's life. *Ed.*

the more we find them to be the men and women who walk in the sunshine. The Luthers, the Wilberforces, the Summerfields, the Guthries, the Spurgeons, and the Norman Macleods,[2] were and are the living illustrations of

2 Some of these names are less well known than others.

John Summerfield (1798-1825) English Methodist preacher and evangelist who ministered in Ireland and (from 1821) the United States, where he was described by one newspaper as 'the modern Whitefield'.See John Holland, *Memoirs of the Life and Ministry of the Rev. John Summerfield, A.M.* (New York: American Tract Society, 1850).

Thomas Guthrie (1803-73), Scottish minister and philanthropist, whom Cuyler met at the General Assembly of the Free Church of Scotland in 1872. A statue erected in his memory on Edinburgh's Princes Street bears the following inscription:

AN ELOQUENT PREACHER OF THE GOSPEL. FOUNDER OF THE EDIN-
BURGH ORIGINAL RAGGED INDUSTRIAL SCHOOLS, AND BY TONGUE
AND PEN, THE APOSTLE OF THE MOVEMENT ELSEWHERE. ONE OF THE
EARLIEST TEMPERANCE REFORMERS. A FRIEND OF THE POOR AND OF
THE OPPRESSED.

BORN AT BRECHIN, FORFARSHIRE. MINISTER SUCCESSIVELY OF ARBIRLOT
AND OF GREYFRIARS AND ST JOHN'S PARISH CHURCHES AND OF FREE
ST JOHN'S CHURCH IN THIS CITY.

Impressions of Guthrie's preaching are given in Iain H. Murray, *A Scottish Christian Heritage* (Edinburgh: Banner of Truth, 2006), p. 320, and in William G. Blaikie, *The Preachers of Scotland* (Edinburgh: Banner of Truth, 2001), pp. 291-292.

Rev. Dr. Norman MacLeod (1812-72). Theologian, prodigious author and social reformer. Born in Campbeltown (Argyll and Bute), the son of a clergyman, MacLeod was brought up in Campsie (East Dunbartonshire). He was educated at the University of Glasgow and completed his studies in Edinburgh under the guidance of Thomas Chalmers (1780-1847). He was appointed minister for Loudoun Parish Church (Ayrshire; 1838-43) and then Dalkeith (1843-45). In 1847, he was a founder of the Evangelical Alliance. In 1851 he accepted the charge of the Barony Church (Glasgow). Horrified by the poverty in this parish he worked hard to improve conditions

the truth that close contact with God is the supremest source of happiness. There is such a thing as 'the joy in the Holy Spirit'. There is a meat for the soul to feed on that this lying, deceitful, and deceived world knows not of. The measure of our holiness is the true measure of our happiness; it will be the measure of our final enjoyment of heaven.

---

for the people. His measures included the extending of the local school, the commencement of evening classes for adults, the establishment of a savings bank, a clothing society, and 'refreshment rooms' to provide good-value food for his parishioners. Macleod was 'a man of enormous capacity for work and considerable personal charisma, an outstanding preacher and a tireless proponent of congregational parochial mission (who) challenges comparison with Chalmers.' *Dictionary of Scottish Church History and Theology* (Edinburgh: T & T Clark, 1993). Macleod is mentioned in Blaikie's *The Preachers of Scotland* (pp. 292-293). *Ed.*

# 18

## THE ANGELS OF THE SEPULCHRE

*I*n In the most beautiful cemetery at the capital of this Commonwealth stands a marble statue carved by the cunning of Palmer's chisel. It represents 'The Angel of the Sepulchre.'[1] On every side the dead are sleeping; but beside them sits this silent sentinel, as if to guard the slumbering dust until the resurrection-trump sounds the *réveille* on the judgment morn. That angel which Palmer's chisel fashioned is of solid stone; but the 'angels in white' whom Mary of Magdala saw in the deserted tomb of Jesus were pure incorporeal spirits. They assumed a visible form; but angels are never described as material beings of flesh and blood like ourselves. Excelling in strength, they go forth as God's messengers to do his will, to watch over children, to bear home the departed spirits of God's people, and to encamp round about his covenant ones who fear him.

[1] Erastus Dow Palmer (1817-1904), a carpenter and self-taught sculptor. His work, 'The Angel of the Sepulchre' was erected in 1865 on the burial plot of Gen. Robert Lenox Banks in Albany Rural Cemetery, New York. *Ed.*

From those angelic appearances at the tomb of our Redeemer on his resurrection morn we may gather some cheering lessons. When the anxious Marys were on their way to that tomb with their spices, the thought flashed into their minds, 'Who will roll away for us that rock at the sepulchre?' But the difficulty is solved in a way that they had not dreamed of. An angel from heaven has already been there, and has opened the gate of rock to let the King of Glory out. So God often sends an angel of help to roll away our hindrances. Some of them are real obstacles; some of them are created by our fears. The awakened sinner often encounters difficulties in a stubborn will, or in long-formed habits, or in obstinate appetites. As soon as he submits to Christ, he finds these difficulties give way: divine power achieves for him what his own unaided weakness could not accomplish.

Many a child of God has been brought under a sore bereavement, and the first thought has been, Oh, how can I bear this burden of grief? How can I surmount all these new hardships and difficulties? A widow left with a brood of orphans, and with scanty provision to feed and clothe them, is tempted to give up in despair. But when she reaches one difficulty after another, lo! the stone is rolled away. A friend provides for this lad; a home is offered to another; a third begins to help himself and mother too and she soon finds that she can do a hundred things which she thought impossible. Beside the widow in her weeds walked an angel in white, which strengthened her.

God always has an angel of *help* for those who are willing to do their duty. How often have we been afraid to undertake some difficult work for him, but as soon as we laid hold of it the rock of hindrance was removed. The tempter told us that if we attempted to save some hardened soul we should encounter an immovable adamant. We had faith enough to try, and prayer brought the power which turned the heart of stone to flesh. Evermore the adversary is busy in frightening us from labours of love for our Master. Yet if our single aim is to reach Jesus and to honour Jesus, no hindrance is immovable. The world thought Paul a madman and Luther a fanatic, and Wilberforce and Duff but pious visionaries.[2] When the omnipotent Help came down, opposing rocks were swept away, and the devil's guards were put to flight. The very lions which frighten—'Mistrust' and 'Timorous'—are discovered to be 'chained' when a persevering Christian comes up to them.

But Help is not the only angel which God sends to his believing ones. There is another bright spirit, whom we

---

2 Alexander Duff (1806-78), pioneer Scottish missionary to India (1830). He visited the US in 1854, receiving an LL.D. from the University of New York. The missionary address he delivered in the Broadway Tabernacle Cuyler described as 'the most overpowering oratory that I ever heard'. Duff was also present at the 1872 General Assembly of the Free Church of Scotland, which Cuyler visited. *Ed.*

never meet more surely than at the sepulchre where our treasures sleep. The name of this angel in white is *Hope*. She sits today by the little mounds that cover the forms we loved. When I go out to the grassy hill in Greenwood, where my darling boy has lain for a dozen summers, I meet that angel at the tomb. The words she chanted when the casket was sealed up and hidden beneath the earth are sounding still: 'All them who sleep in Jesus will God bring with him.' As Mary Magdalene saw the angel through her tears, so the believer sees through tears of sorrow the white-robed angel of Hope. A clear-eyed angel is she, and one that excels in strength. She has other ministering spirits with her to minister to the heirs of salvation. Patience attends her, and Prayer with a casket of promises, and Peace with her serene countenance, and Love, which is stronger than death.

The tomb in Joseph's garden was filled with light where the two bright spirits sat, 'the one at the head and the other at the feet where the body of Jesus had lain'. Even so do the angels of divine help and hope turn the midnight of sorrow into dawn. To the eye of unbelief the grave is a ghostly spot. Faith peoples 'God's acre' with angels, and fills the air with prophetic songs of praise. And what a scene will the Greenwoods and Mount Auburns present when the angelic legions shall roll away every stone, and gather Christ's own chosen ones to meet him on his throne!

Lo! the seal of death is breaking!
Those who slept its sleep are waking,
Heaven ope's its portals fair.
Hark! the harps of God are ringing!
Hark! the seraph's hymns are flinging
Music on immortal air!

# 19

## The Night-Lodging and
## The Day-Dawn

*W*hen travelling in Palestine last year we occasionally came upon a wayside *khan*. Before one of those rude inns the traveller halts at sunset, feeds his beasts, stretches himself on the floor, and in the cool dawn of the next morning saddles his horse or mule and pushes on his journey. This familiar custom was in the Psalmist's mind when he wrote, 'Weeping may endure for a night, but joy cometh in the morning.' This verse literally translated, would read, 'In the evening sorrow lodges, and at the day-dawn comes shouting.' Sorrow is represented as only a lodger for a night, to be succeeded by joy at the sunrising.

This is a truthful picture of most frequent experiences; it is full of comfort to God's people, and it points on to the glorious dawn of heaven's eternal day, when the night-watch of life is over. Sorrow is often the precursor of joy; sometimes it is so needful, that unless we endure the one we cannot have the other. Some of us have known what it is to have severe sickness lodge in our bodily tent, when every nerve became a tormentor and every muscle a highway for pain to course over. We lay on our beds conquered and helpless. But the longest night has its dawn. At length returning health began to steal in upon us, like the earliest gleams of morning light through the window shutters. Never did food taste so delicious as the first meal of which we partook at our own table. Never did the sunbeams fall so sweet and golden as on that first Sabbath when we ventured out to church; and no discourse ever tasted so like heavenly manna as the one our pastor poured into our hungry ears that day. We sang the thirtieth psalm with melody in the heart, and no verse more gratefully than this one, 'Sorrow may endure for a night, but joy cometh in the morning.'

Many a night of hard toil has been followed by the longed-for dawn of success. When we were weary with the rowing the blessed Master came to us on the waves and cried out, 'Be of good cheer; it is I.' As soon as he entered the boat the skies lighted up, and presently the boat was in the harbour. The history of every discovery, of every enterprise of benevolence, of every Christian reform, is the history of toil and watching through long discouragements. I love to read the narrative of Palissy the potter, of his painful struggles with adversity, of his gropings after the scientific truth he was seeking, and of his final victory. Sorrow and poverty and toil lodged with that brave spirit for many a weary month, but at length came singing and shouting. All Galileos and Keplers and Newtons have had this experience. All the Luthers and Wesleys who have pioneered great reformations, and all the missionaries of Christ who have ever invaded the darkness of paganism, have had to endure night-work and watching before the hand of God opened to them the gates of the 'dayspring from on high'. This is the lesson to be learned by us pastors, by the teachers in mission-schools, by colporteurs, and by every toiler for Christ and souls. 'We have toiled all night, and caught nothing', exclaimed the tired and hungry disciples. Then in the early grey of the daybreak they espied their Master on the beach; the net is cast on the right side of the ship, and it swarms with fish enough to break its meshes. Nearly every revival season I have ever passed through in my church has been on this same fashion. Difficulties and discouragements have sent us to our knees, and then we have been surprised by the advent of the Master in great power and blessing. God tests his people before he blesses them. The night is mother of the day; trust through the dark brings triumph in the dawn.

Precisely similar are the deepest and richest experiences of many a regenerated soul. The sorrows of penitence were the precursors of the joys of pardon. I have known a convicted sinner to endure the pangs of contrition when no small tempest lay upon him and no sun or stars appeared; his soul was in the horror of a great darkness. To such distressed hearts God often sends a flood of relief and joy as sudden as the light that poured on Saul of Tarsus. To others conversion has been a slower, gentler process. Like the gradual coming of the dawn—as we have witnessed it from a railway car or from a mountain summit—darkness has slowly given place to steel-grey, and the steel-grey to silver, the silver has reddened into ruddy gold, and all has developed so quietly and steadily that we could not fix the precise birth-moment of the day. Thousands of true Christians cannot fix the precise date of their conversion.[1] But the dawn of hope and new life really begins when the mercy of Jesus Christ is rightly apprehended, and the soul begins to see and to follow him.

> 'Tis midnight with my soul till He,
> Bright Morning Star, bids darkness flee.

Those who suffer the sharpest sorrow for their own sinfulness and guilt, and are brought into the deepest self-loathing, are commonly those who are the most thoroughly converted. The height of their joy is proportioned to the

---

[1] Cuyler testifies to this for himself in his autobiography, *Recollections of a Long Life:* 'I cannot now name any time, day, or place when I was converted. It was my faithful mother's steady and constant influence that led me gradually along, and I grew into a religious life under her potent training, and by the power of the Holy Spirit working through her agency.' *Ed.*

depth of their distress. Christ is all the more precious to them for having painfully felt the need of him. The dawn of their new hope has been unmistakably from heaven, and their after pathway has shone brighter and brighter to the perfect day.

One other truth—the most ineffably glorious of all—is illustrated by this simile of the night-lodging in the *khan*. The earthly life of God's children is only a mere encampment for a night. To many are appointed sleeplessness and tears. Sometimes through poverty, sometimes through long sickness, sometimes under darkly mysterious bereavements, they have 'waited patiently on the Lord more than they that watch for the morning'. They knew that the dawn of heaven lay behind the clouds, and they held out in confident expectation of it. Paul himself had such sharp experiences that he once confessed that he had 'a desire to *break camp* and to be with Christ, which is far better'. A most lovely Christian, whose life had been consumed by a slow cancer, went home to glory a few days ago. While the poor frail tent of the body was decaying by inches, she was feasting on rapturous glimpses of heaven. Through the long weary night pain and suffering lodged in that fluttering tent; but at length

> The dawn of heaven broke—
> The summer morn she sighed for,
> The fair, sweet morn awoke.

## 20

## Our Two Homes

*T*hat beautiful passage in the fifth chapter of the Second Epistle to the Corinthians, according to Dean Alford's and Dr Samuel Davidson's happy rendering, reads about as follows: 'Being always confident, and knowing that whilst we are in our home in the body we are away from our home in the Lord. For we walk by faith, not by appearance. We are still confident, and well content rather to go from our home in the body, and to come to our home in the Lord.'

The contrast is a sharp and distinct one between *our two homes*. In the first verse of this chapter Paul speaks of our present home as a mere 'tent'; the other home is 'a mansion of God eternal in the heavens'. In other words, my soul—which is really myself—has two homes: one of them is in this frail and flimsy tent which I call a body, and the other is in that enduring and glorious habitation called heaven. A tent is the most transient of all lodging-places. It is pitched today; tomorrow its pins are pulled up and the canvas is carried away to some other spot, leaving only the ashes of a camp-fire. What a vivid picture is this of the frail body in which my immortal soul encamps for a few swift-flying years! Half of all the human tents do not last more than thirty years; and if by much mending and patching they are made to last for fourscore years, yet they easily yield to the blast of death and fly away. Paul's tent had seen some rough usage; it was so migratory and so drenched with storms, and so mauled by persecutions and scarred with the lash, that the old hero who lived in it longed 'to depart and to be with Christ, which was far better'. He was constantly getting homesick for his Father's house. A happy day was it for him when the executioner's axe cleaved his poor old leaky tent in two, and suffered his heaven-bound spirit to fly away and be at rest.

A thousand things, speculative and poetical, have been written in regard to the Christian's future home. The Bible says just enough to rouse our curiosity and to stimulate speculation, but not enough to spoil the sublime mystery which overhangs it like a cloud of glory. A few things seem to my own mind at least to be well established. Heaven is a place; it is not a mere state or condition of blissful holiness. A distinctly bounded place of abode it must be, or else John's view of it from Patmos was an idle phantasm. God's Word speaks of it as a 'city', and as filled with 'many mansions'. The light of it proceeds from a central throne; for the Lamb in the midst of the throne is the light thereof. Its pellucid pavements are like unto fine gold. The music of its praises fell upon the old apostle's ear with such a sublime roar of melodies that—likening them to the Mediterranean's surf dashing upon the rocks of Patmos—he calls them 'the sound of many waters'. Surrounding this vast scene of splendour he saw something which he describes as walls of precious stones, and these walls were pierced with gates of pearl.

There is something beautifully suggestive in this many-sidedness of heaven, with gates of entrance from every point of the compass. It emphasizes the catholicity of God's house, into which all the redeemed shall enter, from all parts of the globe, and with their varying theological and denominational opinions. All shall come in through Christ Jesus, and yet through many gateways. Thank God, no bigot shall be able to bar out one soul that has been washed in the blood of the Lamb! The variety of 'fruits' on the tree of life points to the idea of satisfying every possible taste and aspiration of God's vast household of many kindreds and tongues and nations. Why surrender the view of a literal home of the redeemed such as John has described to us? Why volatilize it all away into the thin vapour of metaphor? If John did not see what he described, then he saw nothing at all; and if he saw nothing real, then the closing visions of the Apocalypse are a splendid fog-bank. For one, I prefer to hold to the actual words which Revelation gives me, and if, when I get there, I find something utterly different, then it will be time enough to make the discovery. In the meantime there are millions of us who are simple-hearted enough to fire our faith by singing about those

> Bulwarks with salvation strong,
> And streets of shining gold.

That our heavenly home will satisfy our fullest social longings, we cannot doubt. No one need complain of lack of 'good society' there. Old Dr Emmons is not the only Christian who has fed his hopes of 'a good talk with the Apostle Paul'.[1] Dr Guthrie is not the only parent who has felt assured that 'his little Johnnie would meet him inside the gate.'[2] Many a pastor expects to find his converted flock as a 'crown of rejoicing to him in that day'. The recognition of friends there cannot possibly be a question of doubt. No barriers of caste can separate those who are children of the one Father and dwelling in the same household. When Cineas, the ambassador of Pyrrhus, came back from his visit to Rome in the days of her glory, he reported to his sovereign that he had seen a 'commonwealth of kings'. So will it be in heaven, where every heir of redeeming grace will be as a king and priest unto God,

---

[1] Rev. Dr. Nathaniel Emmons (1745-1840), who ministered at the Congregational Church in Franklin, Mass. *Ed.*
[2] Thomas Guthrie, referred to at the end of chapter 17 (p.99), lost his son Johnnie, an infant of twenty months. *Ed.*

and a divine adoption shall make every one a member of the royal family. What a comforting thought it is that we shall never be compelled to pull up our tent-poles any longer in quest of a pleasanter home! Heaven will have no 'moving-day'. No longer shall we dread to be pulled away from associations which we love, and sent off into strange and uncongenial places. When you and I, brother, have packed up at the tap of death's signal-bell, we shall never be obliged to change our quarters again. There is a delightful permanence in that word, '*Forever* with the Lord.'

The leagues to that home are few and short. Happy is that child of Jesus who is always listening for the footfall this side of the golden gate, and for the voice of invitation to hurry home. A true life is just a tarrying in the tent *for* Christ until we go into the mansion *with* Christ. 'I hope your master has gone to heaven', said someone to a slave when his master was dead. 'I'se afraid he has not gone dare', replied Ben, 'for I never heard him speak of dat. When he go to de North, or de Virginny Springs, he always be gettin' ready for many weeks. I never see him gettin' ready for goin' to heaven.' The simple negro's words are a test and an admonition for each one of us. For let us be assured that not one of us will ever see that home unless we are made ready for it by Christ Jesus.

21

## ASLEEP IN JESUS

*N*o scriptural description of death is so suggestive and so consoling as that which is conveyed by the familiar word *sleep*. It recurs often. Stephen the martyr breathes his sublime prayer, and then 'he fell asleep.' Our Lord said to his disciples: 'Our friend Lazarus sleepeth; but I go that I may awake him out of sleep.' Paul, in that transcendently sublime chapter on the resurrection, treats death as but the transient slumber of the body, to be followed by the glorious awakening at the sound of the last trumpet. And then he crowns it with that voice of the divine Spirit, that marvellous utterance which has been said and sobbed and sung in so many a house of bereavement: 'I would not have you to be ignorant concerning them which are asleep; for, if we believe that Jesus died and rose again, even so them also which sleep in Jesus will God bring with him.' No three words are inscribed on more tombs or on more hearts than these, 'Asleep in Jesus.'

These declarations of God's Word describe death as simply the temporary suspension of bodily activities. Not a hint is given of a total end, an extinction, or an annihilation. The material body falls asleep, the immortal spirit being, meanwhile, in full activity; and the time is predicted when the body, called up from the tomb, shall reunite with the deathless spirit, and the man shall live on through eternity. What we call dying is only a momentary process. It is a flitting of the immortal tenant from the frail tent or tabernacle, which is so often racked with pain and waxes old into decay. Paul calls it a departure: 'To depart and be with Christ.' The spiritual tenant shuts up the windows of the earthly house, ere he departs; he muffles the knocker at the ear, so that no sound can enter; he extinguishes the fire that glows about the heart, stops the warm currents that flow through the veins, and leaves the deserted house, cold, silent, and motionless. We, the survivors, bend over the deserted heart-house; but there is neither voice nor hearing. We kiss the brow and it is marble. The beloved sleeper is sleeping a sleep that thunders or earthquake cannot disturb. But what is there in this slumber of the body that suggests any fear that the ethereal essence of the spirit has become extinct or even suspended its activities? When the mother lays her darling in its crib, she knows that sleep simply means rest, refreshment, and tomorrow morning's brighter eye, nimbler foot, and the carol of a lark in her nursery. When you or I drop off into the repose of the night, we understand that the avenues of the five bodily senses are closed for a few hours; but the mind is, meanwhile, as busy as when we wake.

Death means just this; no more and no less. As Maclaren has vigorously said: 'Strip the man of the disturbances that come from a fevered body, and he will have a calmer soul. Strip him of the hindrances which come from a body that is like an opaque tower around his spirit, with only a narrow crevice here and a narrow door there—five poor senses with which he is connected with the outer universe —and, surely, the spirit will have wider avenues out to God. It will have larger powers of reception, because it has become rid of the closer confinements of the fleshly tabernacle. They who die in Jesus live a larger, fuller, nobler life, by the very cessation of care, change, strife, and struggle. Above all, they live a fuller, grander life, because they "sleep *in Jesus*" and are gathered into his embrace, and wake with him, clothed with white robes, awaiting the adoption—to wit, the redemption of the body.'[1] In God's good time, the slumbering body shall be resuscitated and shall be fashioned like to Christ's glorious body—that is, it shall be transformed into a condition which shall meet the wants of a beatific soul in its celestial

---

[1] Alexander Maclaren (1826-1910). Baptist minister born in Glasgow who held pastorates at Portland Chapel, Southampton (1846-58), and Union Chapel, Manchester (1858-1903), where he became known as 'the prince of expository preachers'. *Ed.*

dwelling-place. Verily, with this transcendent blaze of revelation pouring into the believer's death-chamber and his tomb, we ought not to sorrow as they that have no hope.

In this view of death (which is God's own view) how vivid becomes the apostle's exclamation: 'I am confident and willing rather to be absent from the body and to be present with the Lord.' Who is it that is to be absent? I, Paul—the living Paul—I can be entirely quit from that poor tabernacle of flesh and yet live! My body is no more me than the corn-ship was me when it went to pieces on the shore of Malta and I escaped safe to land. Paul was entirely willing that the old, scarred, and weary body might be put to sleep, so that *he* might go home and be present with his Lord. Then mortality would be swallowed up of life. Go to sleep, poor, old, hard-worked body, the apostle seems to say, and Jesus will wake you up in good time, and you shall be made like to the body of his glory, according to the working whereby he subdues all things unto himself.

Let us not be charged with pushing this Scripture simile too far when we hint that it illustrates the different feelings with which different persons regard the act of dying. When we are *sleepy,* we covet the pillow and the couch. When work is to be done, when the duties of the day are pressing on us, then we are not only broad awake, but the more awake the better. Sleep then is repulsive. Even so do we see aged servants of God, who have finished up their life-work, and many a suffering invalid, racked with incurable pains, who honestly long to die. They are sleepy for the rest of the grave and the home beyond it. Yet desire for death is not natural to the young, the vigorous, or especially to the servants of God who are most intent upon their high calling. These recoil from death, however saintly or spiritual they may be, or however strong be their convictions that heaven is infinitely better than this world. It is not merely the natural shrinking from death (which the man Christ Jesus felt in common with us), but the supreme idea of serving their God to the utmost possible limit. *For* Christ here, *with* Christ yonder, is the highest instinct of the Christian heart. The noble missionary, Judson, phrased it happily when he said: 'I am not tired of my work, neither am I tired of the world; yet, when Christ calls me home, I shall go with the gladness of a boy bounding away from school.'[2] He wanted to toil for souls until he grew *sleepy,* and then he wanted to lay his body down to rest and to escape into glory.

A dying-bed is the only spot where the material frame falls asleep. Then we take up the slumbering form and

[2] Adoniram Judson (1788-1850), American Baptist missionary pioneer to Burma. Between 1812 and his death he laboured in that country, taking only one furlough. An accomplished linguist, he translated the Bible into Burmese. The first Burmese convert was baptised in 1819, but not long after Judson's death, a government survey recorded 210,000 Christians in Burma. *Ed.*

GOD'S LIGHT ON DARK CLOUDS

gently bear it to its narrow bed in mother earth. They who sleep in him shall awake to be forever with their Lord.

On this tremendous question of the resurrection of our loved ones and our reunion with them, our yearning hearts are satisfied with nothing less than *certainty*. Poetic fancies are gossamer; analogies from the sprouting of seeds and bulbs, probabilities, intuitions, and all philosophizings are too shadowy to rear a solid faith on. We demand absolute certainty, and there are just two truths that can give it. The first one is the actual fact of Christ's own resurrection from the death slumber; the second is his omnipotent assurance that all they who sleep in him shall be raised up and be where he is for evermore. Those early Christians were wise in their generation when they carved on the tomb of the martyrs, '*In Jesu Christo obdormivit*' — in Jesus Christ he fell asleep.

The fragrance of this heavenly line perfumes the very air around the believer's resting-place. Giving to the Latin word its true pronunciation, there is sweet melody, as well as heaven-sent truth, in this song of the sleepers:

Oh! precious tale of triumph this!
And martyr-blood shed to achieve it,
Of suffering past - of present bliss.
*'In Jesu Christo obdormivit.'*

Of cherished dead be mine the trust,
Thrice-blessed solace to believe it,
That I can utter o'er their dust,
*'In Jesu Christo obdormivit.'*

Now to my loved one's grave I bring
My immortelle, and interweave it
With God's own golden lettering,
*'In Jesu Christo obdormivit.'*

## 22

# An Autumn Hour in Greenwood

*J*eremy Taylor has quaintly said that it is well for the living to knock often at the gates of the grave.[1] This thought is ever present with me when I thread the walks, and from its many elevations look down into the embowered and shaded vales of Greenwood. The word 'cemetery' signifies a sleeping place; and Greenwood is simply a vast and exquisitely beautiful dormitory, with two hundred and forty thousand slumberers in their narrow beds. Some rest in rosewood beneath roofs of marble; some are laid in the coarse pine box which scanty poverty hides in the bosom of mother earth. But amid all the miscellaneous multitude, the Master knows them that are his; them also which sleep in Jesus will God bring with him.

Yesterday, under a golden October sunshine, I climbed Fountain Hill, and stood amid the fragrant flowers which

[1] *The Rule and Exercises of Holy Dying* (1651). Jeremy Taylor (1613-67), was a royalist clergyman of the Church of England, who after the Restoration of King Charles II, became Bishop of Down and Dromore (Ireland), and also Vice-Chancellor of Trinity College, Dublin. *Ed.*

adorn the bedroom in which my own beloved ones sleep. In that little group lies the beautiful and accomplished daughter, who vanished from the home, of which she was the joy and pride, a twelvemonth ago. Those lips now silent never spoke a disobedient word; the first pang she caused us was when her own noble loving heart ceased to beat. Blessed are such pure hearts, for they shall see God. Never did the spot look more surpassingly lovely, with its immediate canopy of maples tinged with their autumn radiance, and the distant waters of the Bay gilded by the setting sun. The gentle murmurs of the neighbouring fountain seemed like a requiem over the slumberers that were lying closely around. Across the carriage-drive was the arched Gothic tomb in memory of some who sank with the sinking steamer *Arctic* into the ocean depths. Just over an Oak Ridge I could descry the bronze bust of Horace Greeley, with its familiar inscription, 'Founder of the New York Tribune'. Several friends beside whose dying beds I had once stood, were lying in their turf-covered beds beside me. And all over the greensward, and through the crimsoning trees, poured the bright rays of the autumnal sun, kindling the flower-plats into a brilliant glow, and making the very atmosphere glorious as with the anticipated light of the better world.

Standing in that august light I said to myself, So he giveth his beloved *sleep!* Thanks be to him that he takes away the terrors of death from his own redeemed ones by assuring them that death is only a temporary suspension of bodily activities, while the redeemed and immortal spirit has 'departed to be with Christ, which is far better'. Nor shall the slumber of the mortal frame be more than transient. For at the voice of the archangel's trump it also shall awake, and be transformed into that 'spiritual body' which is organized for the peculiar atmosphere and activities of the heavenly state. Then shall Christ's ransomed ones, in their normal and complete condition—body, soul, and spirit—be for ever with their Lord.

I fed my faith by recalling how often God's Word pictures the act of dying as a falling into sleep. I recalled the expression which our Lord employed over the couch of Jairus' daughter, and also his memorable words on the road to Bethany—'Our friend Lazarus is fallen asleep, but I go that I may *awake* him out of sleep.' When Stephen the martyr had uttered his last testimony, and caught his first glimpse of the celestial spheres, he 'fell asleep'. This is the term employed in that magnificent chapter to the Corinthians on the resurrection—a chapter whose single inestimable preciousness is enough to warrant a revelation from heaven. (1 *Cor.* 15) Jesus the conqueror is there described as 'the first fruits'—the earliest harvest sheaf—'of them that are asleep.' As he awakened his slumbering form on the Easter-morn, so shall he awaken those who sleep in Jesus at the resurrection dawn.

This beautiful and comforting conception of dying has

entered into the experiences of multitudes of believers. When the great church historian Neander drew near to his last moment, he sweetly said to his faithful sister: 'Hannchen, I am weary; let us go home; good-night!' One of the aged veterans of the New York pulpit was heard repeating to himself the simple lines of his childhood, as he was departing:

> Now I lay me down to sleep,
> I pray Thee, Lord, my soul to keep.

So have we parents stood beside our darlings and watched the soft dews of kindly slumber steeping the tired eyelids, until there was no longer voice nor hearing. The agony would have been insupportable, if that process meant extinction and remorseless annihilation. But the Son of God was ever saying to us, 'Not dead, but sleeping: them which sleep in me, will I bring with me, that where I am, they shall be also.' Innumerable mothers have stayed up their suffering hearts with this priceless consolation. Somewhere I once met with the following lines, which set forth, touchingly, a mother's caress of the little form that is growing cold in her arms:

> Still she keeps rocking him,
> Ever caressing him,
> Brushing his hair from his colourless brow;
> Softly they've whispered her,
> 'Life has gone out of him;'
> Gently she answers—'how *still* he is now!'

Still she keeps rocking him,
As though she would shake from him
The cold band of death, like the weights from his eyes;
Rocking the *clay* of him,
While softly the soul of him
Angels are rocking far up in the skies.

All these blessed thoughts of the transient sleep and the heavenly waking came to cheer me yesterday as I stood beside the narrow beds covered with tuberoses and geraniums. The setting sun shed its mellow radiance upon green turf and marble tablets, and sparkling fountain. In the distance was the placid Bay with a ship or two resting at anchor—beautiful emblems of a Christian soul whose voyage had ended in the repose of the desired haven. A few birds were twittering their last notes ere they dropped to their perch. The air was as quiet as the dear sleepers beside me, and as I turned from the sacred spot of their slumbers, I bade them as of old *'good-night'*. Beyond these nights of earth, and the last night also, gleams the bright everlasting hope of heaven's 'good *morning!*'

# NOTE

*The following paragraph from the New York Evangelist will explain the circumstances under which this little volume was prepared, and also the peculiar sympathy which the author has with all those who are seeking for God's light on dark clouds of sorrow.*

Died, in Brooklyn, on Friday morning, Sept. 30, 1881, LOUSIE LEDYARD CUYLER, the second daughter of Rev. Theodore L. and Annie E. Cuyler.

On her return from Narragansett Pier in August she was taken with a fever which soon developed typhoid symptoms. After four weeks she rallied, and appeared to be convalescent; but a relapse occurred which baffled the skill of several eminent physicians, and soon proved fatal. During her long illness she sang every day to herself her favourite hymn, 'Abide with me; fast falls the eventide.' It was an early 'eventide' for a beautiful and accomplished young girl, around whom clustered such fond affections and the highest hopes. The constant calls friends at her father's door, for five weeks, and the grief which overspreads the congregation and the community, attest the deep hold which this lovely daughter had laid on so many hearts. Her characteristic traits were perfect simplicity and transparent truthfulness, a playful humour, and at the same time a most conscientious obedience to her parents and to the commandments of her Saviour. At the early age of twenty-one[1] this sweet life, which gave such promise of womanly graces and usefulness, has passed into the life of the better world.

> Out of the pain of night-watching removed
> Into the sleep that God gives his beloved,
> Into the dawn of a glad resurrection,
> Into the house of unbroken affection,
> Into the joy of her Lord—thence confessing
> Death in disguise is his angel in blessing.

[1] In Cuyler's autobiography, *Recollections of a Long Life,* the age of Louise Ledyard Cuyler at death is given as twenty-two. Without a knowledge of her date of birth, we are at a loss to explain this discrepancy. *Ed.*